Reading the
Body Politic

Reading the Body Politic

Feminist Criticism and Latin American Women Writers

Amy K. Kaminsky

University of Minnesota Press
Minneapolis   London

Published by the University of Minnesota Press
2037 University Avenue Southeast, Minneapolis, MN 55414
Printed in the United States of America on acid-free paper

Library of Congress Cataloging-in-Publication Data

Kaminsky, Amy K.
   Reading the body politic : feminist criticism and Latin American women writers / Amy K. Kaminsky.
     p. cm.
   Includes bibliographical references and index.
   ISBN 0-8166-1947-6 (hc).—ISBN 0-8166-1948-4 (pb)
   1. Feminist literary criticism—Latin America.   2. Latin American literature—20th century—History and criticism.   3. Latin American literature—Women authors—History and criticism.   I. Title.
PN98.W64K36 1993
860.9'9287'098—dc20

92-16023
CIP

The University of Minnesota is an
equal-opportunity educator and employer.

For Kenny

Contents

Acknowledgments

In 1984 I moved to Minneapolis and had the extreme good fortune to be invited to join a goup of feminist scholars and writers who met every Friday morning to discuss each other's work. So Sara Evans, Elaine Tyler May, Riv-Ellen Prell, and Cheri Register were there to help when I began writing pieces of what would eventually become *Reading the Body Politic*. They read and thought about what I wrote and gave me advice on how to make it into a book. I am deeply indebted to each of them for their encouragement, their wisdom, their criticism, and their friendship.

Other individuals and organizations have helped me as well. I am grateful to Feministas Unidas, whose MLA panels provided me with an audience and response to the ideas that now appear in several of the following chapters, and to the University of Minnesota and the Bush Foundation for providing the sabbatical leave and financial support that gave me the time and leisure to complete this book. Ongoing conversations with Constance Sullivan and Joanna O'Connell continue to be invaluable to me, and Elaine Dorough Johnson has been a steady source of intellectual and practical assistance. Mercedes de Rodríguez graciously shared materials when they were most needed.

Elizabeth Starčevic and Saúl Sosnowski read and criticized an early draft of the complete manuscript. To the extent to which I have followed their suggestions, my work has been significantly improved. Naomi

Scheman, Beth Jorgensen, Mary Jane Treacy, Jacqueline Zita, and Rebecca Mark commented thoughtfully on individual chapters. Their support and criticism have been a great help to me and almost as gratifying as the wholeheartedly enthusiastic readings of my mother, Florence Katz.

Working with the University of Minnesota Press has been a thoroughly positive experience. I appreciate Biodun Iginla's confidence in my work, Kerry A. Sarnoski's administrative expertise, and Laura Westlund's thoroughness, which is exceeded only by her diplomacy.

Finally, I want to express my appreciation to David and Jonathan Kaminsky who managed to grow to adolescence during the time I wrote this book and almost always got off the computer when I needed to use it, and to Ken Kaminsky who brought the computer into the house in the first place. I thank all three for their humor, their love of language and ideas, and their continuing participation in the feminist critique of almost everything.

Amy Kaminsky
Göteborg, March 19, 1992

Introduction

More than a quarter century ago the Chilean poet Gabriela Mistral wrote that Latin American women no longer feared to write because they had come to possess "the language in abundance." Since Mistral's time the number of women throughout Latin America creating the continent's literary language as they have taken possession of it has multiplied. The critical response to their writing has also grown, although it in no way begins to approach the amount of attention paid to Latin America's men of letters. The Colombian novelist Albalucía Angel has remarked, a little ruefully, that the only people she ever sees reading novels by Latin American women are other women. Certainly the majority of critics who write on texts by women authors are women themselves, and much of the scholarship they produce is an effect, whether direct or indirect, of an international women's movement. Some small percentage of this scholarship on women by women calls itself by the name "feminist criticism," a field of literary scholarship that has been as much a site of conflict as of consensus.[1]

The present volume is part of an international scholarly discussion on feminist literary criticism, as well as a study of a limited number of texts by contemporary Latin American women writers. In its response to the demands of a radical materialist feminism as well as an oppositional politics, the Latin American feminist criticism I am arguing for and practicing here pays attention to both the writer and her texts as producers of meaning within culture. It takes into account gender oppression (closely tied to issues of sexuality) while interacting with the material effects of political and economic dependency and considering the resistance to all of these.

Currently, feminist criticism is becoming more visible to and legitimate among Latin Americanists, and this volume is part of a growing, increasingly self-conscious body of Latin American feminist criticism. Though the culture that gave the world a name for masculine posturing has been resistant to feminism, Latin American literary criticism has begun to give way to the inevitable. Academic *machistas* have denounced, ridiculed, and ignored feminist scholarship—a familiar battery of tactics—but they have not stopped it. Feminist criticism of Latin American texts takes a variety of forms, including feminist analysis of male-authored texts and criticism of texts by women writers. Some feminist critics are writing women's literary history or assembling bibliographies, while others look at the gender bias of literary history and criticism, or at what a Latin American feminist literary criticism might be.[2] Some interview women writers or translate their works.[3] Still others are studying gender itself, especially the interaction between gender ideology and political ideology.[4] The sheer number of women critics drawn to the questions posed by feminist criticism, as well as the vanguard of men secure enough in their own masculinity and intellectual ability so as not to be threatened by feminism, has created a space for feminist literary criticism in journals and conferences, and, more recently, in monographs.

This sea change may be best understood in all its ambiguity in Roberto González Echevarría's assessment of Sharon Magnarelli's *The Lost Rib*. González Echevarría names Magnarelli's book as one of the most insightful and original works of contemporary Latin American literary criticism, but in his discussion of *The Lost Rib* he does not allude to feminism, even indirectly. Whether this extremely knowledgeable and accomplished critic is aware that Magnarelli's work is feminist scholarship and has chosen, chivalrously, to avert his glance from her immodest display, or whether he really does not recognize feminist criticism when he sees it, is probably of little consequence. Both attitudes derive from the same male-centered source and suggest that perhaps the Latin American critical establishment will embrace feminist scholarship if we are modest and discreet and call it something else.[5] The growing visibility of feminist criticism is both a cause and an effect of an increasing respectability that may well dull its edge, and the very success of academic feminist work may provide the means to dampen feminism's radicalism.[6]

Paying attention to women writers or to the image of women in literature without engaging the power imbalance inherent in gender relations, for example, promises not to question the ground of traditional analysis. The acceptability of such criticism merely opens the door to a few well-mannered women who will not forget their proper place. Insofar as this kind of scholarship unreflexively accepts the ideological underpinnings of the text, its inevitable outcome is the reinscription of traditional gender patterns. The dazzling theorizing of post-Freudian psychoanalytic criticism, on the other hand, threatens to do away with women altogether and substitute a notion of the feminine that relies on conventional (not to mention heterosexist) notions of woman as mother that can be embodied in any literary text, no matter the gender of its author. This approach often strays far enough from the issues of the material oppression of women that it loses sight of such concerns. Finally, the politically engaged criticism that welcomes feminism as an allied struggle often recognizes gender oppression only as a subcategory of class (or sometimes racial) oppression, which remains first on the agenda. I do not wish to discard, wholesale, any of these approaches. Noticing the presence of women in literature is a useful first step in creating a feminist criticism; psychoanalytic theory has provided feminists with useful analytic tools; and as a Latin Americanist, I am committed to a feminist analysis that engages issues of class, race, and geopolitics. But it is necessary to assert that gender oppression is not merely an effect of capitalism or colonialism and that feminist scholarship needs to keep women firmly at the center of its analysis.

Specifically, feminist scholarship needs to retain the notion of sexuality as a key to gender hierarchy and therefore as a site of oppression, without pushing women back into the little corner in which they are nothing but sex and have nothing to say about anything but sex. For though self-critical feminist theory has in recent years incorporated into its analysis the specificities of class, race, and nationality that inform and shape the oppression of women, in most feminist accounts, sexuality remains a constant of women's subordination.[7] Whether it is the will to fix paternity and thus rights of inheritance in the aristocracy, the sexual use of female slaves throughout history, the obsessive drive to contain what is perceived as female excess, or the categorizing of women's work as reproductive rather than productive, what is specific to women's oppression is the impulse to regulate female sexuality, which in turn depends on the enforcement of heterosexuality.[8] The resulting polarized and rigid, gender-identified sexuality runs so deep that it has been used as a metaphor in ascribing meaning to such diverse phenomena as imperialism and electrical wiring. The radical recovery of women's sexuality that lesbian feminism implies, then, is profoundly political, as well as crucial to an understanding of discursive practice.

Discussions of sexuality get particularly sticky in Latin American criticism when lesbianism surfaces as an issue, however. At the moment, virulent heterosexism accommodates homophobia on the right, where lesbianism (like male homosexuality) is seen as a sin born of permissiveness, and on the left, where it is characterized as bourgeois decadence. Alternatively, lesbian sex is dismissed out of hand as "not sex" since no penis is involved, or, perhaps most insidious of all, as mental illness.[9]

Given phallocratic culture's will to control women's sexuality, it is not surprising that sexual expression on the part of women that does not include men is the most forbidden of all. It is still possible to silence potentially feminist women with the epithet "lesbian."[10] Heterosexuality is so deeply ingrained that it is passed off not only as "natural" but as the *sole* natural expression of sexuality. To be called "lesbian" is to be called "monster." One of the reasons that academic feminism (which might be defined as the intellectual legitimation of feminist thought) is so slow to grow in Latin America and practically nonexistent in its literary criticism and theory, is women scholars' fear of having their sexuality impugned. Yet for feminists to comply with the taboo on lesbianism is to hand antifeminists a convenient device with which to frighten us into submission. Until women are no longer terrorized by the threat of the mark of deviance whenever they shift their glance from the male cultural project, as long as women fear being called lesbians for giving their energy and attention to other women, feminist criticism will be crippled.[11] Consequently, the feminist critical project ignores lesbian theory and criticism at its peril.

Moreover, a literary criticism that takes as one of its goals the transformation of repressive cultural practice, as both feminist literary criticism and Latin American materialist literary criticism do, needs to take into account that which is most repressed and most forbidden. This project not only opens the culture to as full a view as possible but also stands to liberate those subjects relegated to invisibility.

At least since the "Boom" of the late 1960s, when Latin American literature entered the international market and became a prestigious cultural commodity, its writers and critics have claimed that naming, defining, shaping, and challenging Latin America is a primary function of the literature of the continent. Mario Vargas Llosa's famous early pronouncement that the unwieldiness of Latin American history and experience virtually requires its novelists to create the continent in their texts, is echoed (in ways he now might disavow) in the testimonial narrative of writers like Alicia Partnoy, whose texts are meant to spur her readers to action. Similarly, the richest vein of Latin American criticism is the politically committed work of such critics as Angel Rama and Jean Franco.[12]

In the United States, however, politically partisan literature, perhaps to an even greater degree than politically committed criticism, is suspect. Though feminist theory here has demonstrated the interdependence of the public and private realms and shown how self and other are not mutually exclusive, it still has not sufficiently questioned the extent to which "political" and "aesthetic" have been constructed as antithetical. Hardnosed politicians in this country sneer at what they construe as the indecisiveness and escapism of the artistic imagination.[13] Scholars of literature, on the other hand, tend—like their compatriots—to reduce politics to the electoral process. Furthermore, they think of political discourse as necessarily simpleminded. Overt allegiance to a political movement or party, particularly in a writer, seems naive and gauche. North Americans do not know what to make of a writer whose content is political and whose language is supple, since we have learned to believe that attachment to political ideals turns language rigid. But language does not congeal into rhetoric on the basis of subject matter, nor does commitment to change by means of group action in the public realm (which is essentially what I mean by "politics" here) subject a writer to spiritual, emotional, or aesthetic poverty. When North American feminists made the extraordinary theoretical discovery that the personal was the political—that the intimate lives of individuals responded to cultural structures of hierarchy and dominance, they did not stop to consider to what extent the political might also be the personal: that the public institutions housing and channeling and deploying state power express themselves in our individual lives. In much of Latin America, the official and unofficial policies of the state are played out on the bodies of its citizens, thus becoming the intimate personal experience and shaping the unique vision of the individual that gets expressed in what we recognize as the writer's particular voice.

Just as Latin American feminist criticism needs to make room for readings of sexuality that go beyond labeling and dismissal, it must take the
political, in all its complexity, into account.

1

Translating Gender

It came as no surprise to speakers of more than one language when theorists noted that language was not a transparent vehicle for the expression of reality. Words and experience create each other within culture, and what should be the most direct line from one language to another, what we call "literal translation," in fact connotes incompleteness of meaning. Furthermore, the slippage that occurs when we shift from one language to another does not take place in a cultural and political vacuum. In the United States, translation occurs within the constraints of hegemonic notions of particular languages, attached to particular cultures. English in the United States often apologizes for not getting French quite right, but it never assumes such a subordinate attitude toward Spanish. The racism and xenophobia that results in this country's devaluation of the Spanish language also devalues the thinking that is expressed in that language.[1] This would be an important issue in any case for feminist scholars working between English and Spanish, but it is exacerbated by the fact that the words having to do with sex and gender—crucial categories of analysis for feminist theory—differ radically in meaning and application in English and Spanish.

Feminist theorists from the United States have become accustomed to assuming a difference between sex and gender that, broadly speaking, places the former in the realm of nature and the latter in the realm of culture. What has been useful for English-speaking feminist critics in the sex/ gender differentiation is the ability to put a name to a distinction that was once not ordinarily perceived. Gender had been naturalized; common sense said that mothers were better at caring for babies than fathers, and that boys were better at mathematics than girls. These notions are no longer self-evident. Quite the contrary: they now appear to be part of a pernicious ideology so pervasive that it once had us all convinced. The distinction between sex—the biological given—and gender—what culture fashions out of that division—helped us recognize this, and it is a distinction that we are loath to let go. "Gender" has superseded the sociological term "sex role," a phrase that, although capturing the social and cultural overlay in the behaviors expected of men and women, remains on the surface of behavior and expectations, without facilitating an analysis of the structures that produce them. "Gender," on the other hand, is a category of analysis, like class. For that reason it is such a crucial concept for feminist theorists.

The term "gender," referring to a category of social and cultural rather than grammatical difference, has no ready counterpart in Spanish, despite the apparent cognate, *género*. This lack has marked a division between feminist literary critics whose native language is Spanish who write primarily in Spanish, and those whose original tongue is English.[2]

For Teresa de Lauretis, the untranslatability of the English "gender" bodes ill for what she sees as the project of "[espousing] an internationalist, not to say universal, view of the project of theorizing gender."[3] Yet it is precisely the uncoupling of "internationalist" from "universal" that promises to make such theorizing possible. Feminism in its less parochial versions opposes the uniformity of universalism, which has always repressed difference. To be politically and analytically successful, feminism must be inclusive, which means, among other things, international, even if precise definitions and uniform goals are then beyond our grasp. I am in full agreement that our lack of a shared terminology is a serious problem, since, like de Lauretis, I believe that such an absence is no mere aberration, but rather a representation of a profoundly held essentialist understanding in Romance cultures of the nature of what North American feminists would call gender. On the other hand, the category we call gender is turning out to be valid for at least some Latin American feminist scholars, who are in the process of finding a language to accommodate it.

The sex/gender distinction in English, although establishing gender as a cultural construction, can, however, serve to embed sex in nature. Some thinkers have therefore gone beyond the distinction and have all but collapsed the two terms by claiming that both are equally constructed. Others deconstruct the notion of "nature" itself.[4] Some Swedish feminist theorists, whose language, like Spanish, has a single word, *kön,* to designate both sex and gender, claim that the English distinction is in fact false and enables the culture to maintain that beyond gender there is an essential, biological difference between men and women.[5] I do not believe that Latin American feminists are cultural constructionists in the same way these Swedes are, but the possibility that the word *sexo* might denote difference as constructed in culture has not been fully appreciated by North American feminists for whom the cognate "sex" has seemed irredeemably tied to biology.

Though we might not concede that the sex/gender division will work in most Hispanic contexts, it is still useful to be able to express the distinction, if only to make North American feminist theory comprehensible in Latin America. Whether North American notions of what Gayle Rubin called the sex-gender system, or what others have defined simply as gender (as opposed to sex), are valid theoretical tools for discussing Latin American structures, institutions, and experience is another, albeit central, question.

To address it, North American feminists must confront ethical and political questions, as well as our epistemology. Traditional scholarship simply imposes the analytical categories central to its own intellectual enterprise when these have no counterpart in the field of study. Feminist theory has resisted this sort of imposition, demonstrating how such a practice can distort the object of study and occlude some of its crucial elements. For feminists, therefore, it is highly problematic for those in a position of power (the researcher, the North American) to claim the superiority of their own terminology over the terminology of those in a subdominant position (the researched, the Latin American). Feminist theory is grounded in a political practice and an ethical imperative that abhors hierarchy and deconstructs power relations. The paradox of imposing an alien theoretical system on an already subordinate group is not lost on feminist theorists. The decision to adhere to such a system can only come from within. North American feminists can only offer their example, to be used or modified freely by Latin American feminists. The troublesome word here is "freely," since women, even feminist women, as well as men are subject to hegemonic beliefs that may well influence their choices.

Speaking from a subordinate position, the position feminists are used to occupying, offers both moral and epistemological support to one's analysis. The disempowered have earned their right to speak, and they have been required, as the powerful have not, to understand the workings of the systems of the powerful in order to survive. Feminists in North America may be disempowered within their own culture, where they learned these reading skills, but they are far from disempowered with respect to their objects of study when these are from the developing world.

Because of the reality of cultural imperialism and the resistance of North American feminists to practice it and of Latin American theorists on the left to permit it, the forgoing of translation altogether in favor of the English term "gender" is an untenable solution to the terminology problem. At a time when Latin America is struggling against North American neocolonialism, the introduction of a North American term into a radical discourse is both undesirable and virtually impossible to achieve. Among literary theorists, who both revere and mistrust language, this problem is exacerbated. Their mistrust of the political implications of any new meaning to be assigned to *género* is reinforced by a reverence for the term's original linguistic and literary meaning, which, as it turns out, is not shared by social scientists. But also, perhaps, the rejection of *género* as it is used in English legitimates refusing feminism as a theory, and particularly of refusing what seems to be a bourgeois, North American version of feminism.[6]

It is necessary to disentangle the fear of feminism itself (which leads to uneasiness with feminism's jargon) from what is for me a more legitimate disfavor with the term *género*. The problem with the word lies in *género's* preexisting "strong meaning," which fills the word's semantic space in a way that the English "gender" was not so occupied. Originally "gender" in English referred only to grammatical categories, but English nouns have no gender, except secondarily and in limited ways (the ship = she, for example), or except where the nouns signify something male or female. "Gender," even in its underutilized grammatical sense, attaches to sex, providing the link that made the term readily available for making sense of the cultural constructs that surround and are women and men. In Spanish, however, *género* already carried two meanings, both having to do with other sorts of categorization and difference: grammatical gender and literary or artistic genre. The former is sometimes related to femaleness or maleness, but the other is not except in the most remote and artificial kind of way.[7]

The strong meanings of English "gender" and Spanish *género* are, then, quite different. It was relatively easy for gender to be detached from its meaning as a grammatical term in English (since it did not speak to the immediacy of English speakers in their own language), but grammatical difference *is* the strong meaning in Spanish. In Spanish, moreover, the genders are called masculine and feminine, not neuter and nonneuter as in some other languages, so even the words *masculino* and *femenino* have meanings not attached to embodiment or sexuality. In Spanish the strong meaning for *género* is not primarily connected to embodied, culturally constructed differences between men and women, though that connection is not completely severed. The words *masculino* and *femenino* are also strongly and weakly defined, although they attach more strongly to male/female and the string of terms having to do with people and social relations than does the term *género*, which does not carry in itself the male/female (as differentiated from the masculine/feminine) dichotomy.

The relationship between the strong and weak meanings of *género* can be illustrated by looking at particular lexical items. Although there is nothing in *la silla* that marks it female (I use this term instead of feminine to exaggerate the connection between biology and constructed femininity) or in *el televisor* to mark it male, certain words' grammatical gender coincides with a semantic notion of maleness or femaleness (*el hombre, la mujer,* most obviously). Other lexical items are grammatically one gender though ambiguous semantically, depending on the context (*el modelo, la persona*), and others are grammatically one and semantically the other (*la patria*). To pose the question, What is the gender of *la patria*? / ¿Cuál es el género de la patria?, is to ask two different questions. For the English speaker, the word "gender" refers first and foremost to the semantic content of the word, as it connotes notions of fatherland, patriarchy, and a particular set of political and social relations. *La patria* is gendered masculine through etymology and because of the emotional, historical, and interpersonal charge it bears. In Spanish, the semantic content of the term is, traditionally, as masculinely loaded as it is in English, while the gender of the lexical item, *la patria*, is undisputedly feminine. Another gendered term with a similar meaning, *la tierra* (earth, land), retains a feminine semantic as well as grammatical charge. *La tierra* nourishes, sustains, is prior to transformation by politics, economics, technology. One loves *la tierra*, is loyal to *la patria*. The phrase *madre tierra* (mother earth) rolls off the tongue, while *patria* is rooted in the notion of the father. These are old dichotomies, discussed and contested by North American feminists for the past twenty years, facilitated by a terminology that allows for a notion of culturally constructed gender adhering to people, actions, objects, and abstractions. For the English speaker, gender derives from the body and can depart from it, although it always retains some form of that early connection. For the Spanish speaker, the grammatical femininity of the word *patria* makes it possible to ignore the semantic connection in favor of the morphological one. Shifting the meaning of *patria* from masculine to feminine can be a powerful discursive tactic. This has been done in at least two cases, and both have strong political implications. In the song "Madre," by Angel and Isabel Parra, the word "mother" is reconstructed to encompass nation and revolution: *madre patria y madre revolución* (mother country, mother revolution), contesting the meaning of both terms in each phrase.[8] In another instance, Luisa Valenzuela translates *patria* as "motherland," refiguring the underlying meaning of the term.[9]

Gender's persistent connection to body, and the occasional feminist desire to suppress that connection, can be discerned in a sentence I once wrote in which I made reference to the term "writer" as a gender-free category: "Since so many women who have written have disappeared from accounts of the literature, those who have come after them claim presence in the apparently gender-free category, 'writer.' " Yet it is patently untrue that the word "writer" is not gendered, even if in English it is unmarked. Spanish unmasks this apparent neutrality. *Escritor* is, grammatically, a masculine noun. That it is also semantically masculine is revealed by the use of a feminized form, *escritora,* to refer to a woman who writes. Furthermore, differential value is attached to feminine forms of nouns, when grammatical gender follows embodied, social gender. The word *poetisa* is still much more common in Spanish than "poetess" in English, and only minimally less pejorative; *la poeta* still rings wrong to many.[10] Some grammatical formations seem to refuse women's participation in certain activities. There is no elegant term for the woman critic: *la crítica* is criticism itself, and *el crítico* clearly is a man, a case of grammatical gender ratifying historical precedent. We are left with grammatically and stylistically unsatisfying locutions such as *la mujer crítico.* In fact, many feminist critics prefer to define themselves with the ambiguous term *la crítica,* refusing to be gendered masculine. Other feminized forms referring to professions have changed meaning entirely, in order to reflect changing cultural practice. *La doctora* no longer means "the doctor's wife," but the doctor herself.

Género's strong grammatical meaning in Spanish makes the term less accessible to theorists who would use it in its English sense. If it were adopted, it would carry an even stronger connotation of the arbitrary nature of gender, making the adoption all the less likely, for being counter-intuitive. In Latin America gender still appears natural and not constructed, certainly not arbitrary.

Given the cultural resistance to a notion of a *culturally constructed* difference between men and women and the strong grammatical meaning of *género* that functions to obscure any other, it should not be surprising that *género* resists identification with "gender." One might wish for another word altogether, but there does not appear to be one that carries with it the notion of constructed difference out of perceived biological binarism. A similar problem exists in French, but its high status as a theoretical language has likely kept American feminists from raising the embarrassing possibility of a paucity of nuance in that language. It may well be that some of the apparent essentialism and conservatism of French feminist theory derives from and is expressed by not having a word for gender useful beyond the grammatical. *Le sexe,* like *el sexo,* is almost automatically recuperated by essentialism. Even so, writers like Luce Irigaray, Hélène Cixous, and Monique Wittig have been much more iconoclastic in their treatment of language than have Spanish American feminists.

Rather than reassessing the rejection of essentialism (which may be implicit in U.S. feminists' reluctance to impose a theoretical structure on their Latin American subjects of study), we might look at linguistic constructs that suggest that what essentializes gender in English might not do so in Spanish.[11] If *género* has nothing to do with "gender" understood as cultural constructedness of people in relation to sex, for example, it might also be the case that "sex" has no real cognate counterpart either. Though at present *sexo* functions to collapse sex and gender, naturalizing and essentializing both, it is potentially the Swedish *kön,* i.e., a constructed sexuality/sex/gender.

Like the word "gender," the use of the abstract singular term "woman" only appears to be congruent in Spanish and English. In recent years, "woman" has been abandoned by North American feminists for being a totalizing, essentializing term that denies the specificity of different women in particular historical (class, race, national, ethnic, religious) contexts.[12] This is so much the case that any text in English that speaks of "woman" rather than "women" immediately signals itself to be anti-feminist or hopelessly naive. The usage of the singular *la mujer,* however, while also carrying that generalizing force in Spanish, does not foreclose on difference among women to the same extent that "woman" has come to do in English. In the following passage, for example, *la mujer,* singular and apparently abstract, is far from being the ahistorical creature incapable of thought, change, or political purpose:

> Sin duda alguna la mujer, desde hace mucho tiempo, ha venido reflexionando sobre su situación y planteando reivindicaciones que le provean la oportunidad de superar un papel enmarcado en esquemas culturales, sociales y económicos.

> [Without a doubt, woman has, for a very long time, been thinking about her situation and positing revindications that might provide her with the opportunity of overcoming a defined role in cultural, social, and economic designs.][13]

The feminist tone of this passage, as well as its clear sense of process and historical change, belies any essentializing tendency that the English use of the abstract singular imparts. A good translation of this passage would render the Spanish singulars plural in English.

Similarly, the adjective *femenino* cannot simply be translated as the always already corrupt "feminine," since it also functions to connote "that which pertains to women."[14] "Women's writing," for example, is ordinarily translated as *literatura femenina,* even by feminist critics. *Femenino*'s two meanings do not occur independently of each other, but rather are in constant articulation. The use of *femenino* by feminist critics has, therefore, not gone unnoted or uncontested. Lucía Guerra Cunningham rejects the possibility of a value-free use of the adjective; for her it always carries a pejorative charge. Eliana Rivero, on the other hand, is ambivalent about the use of the word, wanting to rescue it for Hispanic feminist use yet also recognizing the danger in reclaiming a word within a discursive context that still insists on its old meanings. Rivero's impulse to rescue *femenino* is predicated on her resistance to the anglicizing reading of the word as always and only pejorative. That is, she means to claim the specificity of Spanish meaning that must underlie any particularly Spanish American feminism and to maintain the difference between English and Spanish in order to avoid a neocolonial feminism.

To a great extent, however, the Spanish-speaking feminists who are interrogating their language have been influenced by feminist theorists in other languages who have undertaken the same task. Moreover, much

Latin American feminist literary analysis is being written—or at least being published—in the United States. Academic feminist scholarship in Latin America occurs most often in the social sciences rather than in the humanities, and on the whole Latin American feminism tends to be extraacademic. Both Rivero and Guerra Cunningham, for example, live and work in the United States; they are familiar not only with the fundamental questioning of language by North American feminists, but also with French feminism's reclamation of the discursive feminine. Of the theorists working in Latin America, the most linguistically radical is the Argentine Lea Fletcher, whose first language was not Spanish. The literary critics writing in Spanish who use the term *género* to discuss English "gender" tend to be those trained in the United States. This is not surprising, since the writer's proximity to both English usage and U.S. feminist meanings encourages some form of approximation in Spanish. On the other hand, there is a competing impulse for expatriate or exiled literary scholars. Their resistance to *género* as "gender" can be understood in terms of the political and psychological stake in maintaining their native language as they knew it.

Still, some Latin American feminist scholars do use the word *género* in the way that English speakers use "gender." Most of these are social scientists, whose disciplinary jargon may make the transition easier. Sociologists, for example, began using the term gender, translated as *género* and meaning something like sex, earlier in the century. The term was, then, implanted in their discipline, ready for later feminist appropriation and refinement. Julieta Kirkwood, a sociologist, and Ana Vásquez, a psychoanalyst, both from Chile, have written extensively about feminism, and both use the term *género* without qualm. Kirkwood refers to "la discriminación y subordinación del género, la jerarquía y disciplina de este orden denominado 'natural', que más tarde será proyectado a todo el acontecer social" ["the discrimination and subordination of gender, the hierarchy and discipline of this so-called 'natural' order, that later will be projected upon everything that happens in the social realm"]. Shortly thereafter she modifies *género* to make it clear that she is speaking of the sex/gender system:

Esto nos lleva a constatar que hay dos áreas o ámbitos de acción en relación a lo político, tajantemente separados y excluyentes entre sí, en virtud de los géneros sexuales. (64)

[This brings us to affirm that there are two areas or spheres of action in relation to the political, absolutely separate and mutually exclusive, by virtue of the sexual genders.][15]

In an earlier article, "El feminismo como negación del autoritarismo" (Feminism as negation of authoritarianism), Kirkwood also uses the term *género* to express a relationship that is purely and socially constructed:

> Para el análisis feminista sin embargo, empezó a ser evidente que la razón de ser del autoritarismo o conservatismo femenino no radicaba en "esencias" femeninas, sino que por el contrario, obedecía a una "razón de género" y por lo tanto a una pura construcción social, cultural y política, cuyos parámetros eran otros, apenas atisbados. (146)

> [For feminist analysis, however, it began to be evident that the reason for women's conservatism or authoritarianism did not lie in feminine "essences," but rather the opposite; it obeyed a "law of gender" and therefore a pure social, cultural, and political construction whose parameters were other ones, barely scrutinized.][16]

Ana Vásquez writes, "hemos aprendido que, como género histórica-mente dominado, carecemos (mejor dicho, hemos sido desposeídas) de los instrumentos y las estructuras conceptuales que debieran permitirnos entender nuestra situación" (56) ["we have learned that, as a historically dominated gender, we lack (rather, we have been dispossessed of) the in-struments and conceptual structures that should have allowed us to un-derstand our situation"].[17] Here Vásquez lights on a crucial concern for feminists: the need for a language appropriate to express our experiences, ideas, theories, and aspirations. At the same time, in the context of Latin America, a conscious attempt has been made by writers and critics to claim a particularly American language (and more specifically, particu-larly national and regional languages). For neither feminists nor Latin American writers has language ever been a simple matter of transpar-ency.[18]

Latin American feminist theorists have remained fairly conservative in their use of language, unlike feminists of postmodernism, writing under the sign of deconstruction, and radical feminists gleefully claiming a lan-guage. Latin American political and literary theorists, however, have been painfully conscious of the struggle to create a language that is not sub-servient to a colonial past and neocolonial present. Here they coincide with feminists worldwide who, as Ana Vásquez points out, "hemos dado cuenta de que incluso el lenguaje—vehículo de las ideas—ha sido elabo-rado por otros, para expresar una visión de la realidad que no es la nuestra, sus estructuras no nos convienen y para la mayoría de nosotras son incluso incomprensibles" (56) ["we have realized that even language—the vehicle of ideas—has been elaborated by others, to express a vision of reality that is not ours; its structures do not meet our needs and for the majority of us are even incomprehensible"].

To meet the challenge of androcentric language, Julieta Kirkwood relaxes the rules of grammatical gender in ways that most literary theorists do not:

> Por una parte, incorpora a lo político el ámbito de la "necesidad" y, por otra parte, se incorpora a las mujeres como "nuevas sujetas" o "actoras" de la política, en tanto objeto sobre el que recaía el mundo de la necesidad. ("Feministas y políticas" 65)
>
> [On the one hand, it incorporates into the political the sphere of "necessity" and, on the other hand, women are incorporated as "new subjects" or "actors" in politics, insofar as they are the object on which the world of necessity devolves.]

Kirkwood takes a matter-of-fact, practical attitude toward this problem. She stretches the limits of language, bends a few rules, and creates an adequate language through which to express herself. Kirkwood uses the form *actora,* the woman as political actor, which will probably find little argument. It is an elegant term, distinguishing between theatrical and social actors (*actriz* and *actora*), and has its analogues in other feminized words, like *escritora. Nuevas sujetas,* however, is a defiant term, breaking the strict grammatical rule that separates human sex/gender from grammatical gender in words like *modelo, víctima, persona, objeto.* This term, with its adjectival echoes, puns on the freedom and agency associated with subjectivity and the bondage of the woman who is "subject to" another. The force of the neologism, and its self-contained oxymoron, are underscored by the use of the word *objeto* in the same sentence, referring to the same female subject but in its grammatically masculine form. Kirkwood is not particularly given to the radical wordplay of writers like Mary Daly or Hélène Cixous; her prose tends to be undiluted sociologese. When she uses words in an unusual way, it is not to produce a smile of delight and recognition in her reader, but rather to find an adequate linguistic form for the ideas she wishes to express. Kirkwood is not troubled by the question of the transparency of language. Unlike deconstructionist feminists who are fully aware of the treachery of language, Kirkwood and other feminist writers grounded in Marxism use language as a handy tool, like laboratory scientists who jerry-rig a new piece of equipment to handle a new technique or do a new experiment. Kirkwood is not in awe of language; it is there to do the job, and where it falls short, the speaker simply gets to invent a new term. Even so, Kirkwood encloses her neologisms in quotation marks, signaling their difference.

Similarly, feminists writing on literature outside the academy seem less constrained by linguistic norms. Raquel Olea, writing in the feminist poetry review *Palabra de mujer*, disobeys rules of grammatical gender somewhat differently from Kirkwood, rendering the female subject *la sujeto*, maintaining the original masculine ending but signaling a feminine referent by means of the definite article. In the same issue of the review, the Argentine feminist Lea Fletcher proposes a new third person neuter plural. Given language's tendency toward conservatism in syntax, as opposed to semantics (new nouns and verbs enter Spanish with some dispatch; new pronouns and verb forms do not), this innovation has little chance of being accepted. Yet its proposal is testimony to the constraints women feel within the language.

Feminist literary critics in academia, with their more burdened relationship to language, find themselves trapped in grammatical structures that undermine their political and theoretical stance. Patricia Pinto Villarroel, a Chilean like Kirkwood, offers a painful example. She is unable to follow the sociologist's lead in appropriating and feminizing old masculine nouns. Instead, she uses the masculine form, explaining her "choice" in a long and agonizing footnote that quite clearly expresses the violence language does to women and the way it deforms feminist thought:

> La tradición lingüística me obliga a usar el género masculino para referirme a un sujeto de enunciación femenino. La violencia que me producía escribir *la* sujeto me hizo rendirme ante el peso de la norma. Quede este pequeño drama como ejemplo de uno de los múltiples obstáculos con que tropezamos las mujeres cuando intentamos hablar de nosotras con un lenguaje que, al menos en cierto grado, literalmente no nos pertenece y nos traiciona o nos oculta. (66, n. 6)

> [Linguistic tradition obliges me to use the masculine gender to refer to a feminine subject of enunciation. The violence that I felt upon writing "the subject" [as a feminine noun] made me yield to the weight of the norm. Let this little drama remain as an example of the multiple obstacles against which we women stumble when we try to speak of ourselves with a language that, at least to some degree, literally does not belong to us and betrays us or conceals us.][19]

This is the language of defeat and victimization, of a woman caught in the language that speaks her. Pinto's sophisticated analysis coupled with her anguish at being unable to express it in the body of her text suggests the complexity of the problem. That she cannot now, and may never be able to, defy her language returns us to the ethical/political question of the North American feminist Latin Americanist who would utilize the word "gender" to name her primary analytic category, and Teresa de Lauretis's intimation that there can be no internationalist feminist theorizing of gender unless (until) all languages can express the notion of gender in relation to sex. Right now, what we have to deal with is a multiplicity of terms meeting singly and in combination around notions of sex, gender, grammar, and representation. It may be that this will enrich our theorizing, just as questioning the unadorned singular, "woman," has wrested feminist theory in English out of its monism, forcing recognition of the different ways in which one is a woman, depending on race, class, ethnicity, age, sexuality. Feminist theory, even (especially?) in the United States, now knows that gender is never unmodified, and the struggle to locate gender within the constraints of different kinds of social organization stands to strengthen our theory, as well as complicate our task. My own use of the term "gender" in the following chapters is rooted in the northern soil of U.S. feminism, but flowers in the southern light of Latin America.

2

Gender as Category and Feminism as Strategy in Latin American Literary Analysis

Patria, mi patria, vuelvo hacia ti la sangre.
Pero te pido, como a la madre el niño
lleno de llanto.
    [Country, my country, I turn my blood toward you.
    But I am begging you like a child begs his mother,
    filled with tears.]

La Compañía Frutera, Inc.
se reservó lo más jugoso,
la costa central de mi tierra,
la dulce cintura de América.
    [The United Fruit Company, Inc.
    kept for itself the juiciest part,
    the central coast of my land,
    the sweet waist of America.]

                      Pablo Neruda[1]

En efecto, toda mujer, aun la que se da voluntariamente, es desgarrada, chingada por el hombre. En cierto sentido todos somos, por el solo hecho de nacer de mujer, hijos de la Chingada, hijos de Eva. Mas lo característico del mexicano reside, a mi juicio, en la violenta, sarcástica humillación de la Madre y en la no menos violenta afirmación del Padre. ... Si la Chingada es una representación de la Madre violada, no me parece forzado asociarla a la Conquista, que fue también una violación, no solamente en el sentido histórico, sino en la carne misma de las indias.

[In effect, all women, even those who give themselves voluntarily, are torn open, fucked by men. In some sense we are all, simply by virtue of having been born of woman, sons of *la Chingada*, sons of Eve. But what is characteristic of the Mexican lies, to my way of thinking, in the violent, sarcastic humiliation of the Mother and the no less violent affirmation of the Father. . . . If *la Chingada* is a representation of the raped Mother, it does not seem forced to me to associate her with the Conquest, which was also a rape, not only in the historical sense, but also in the very flesh of Indian women.]

Octavio Paz[2]

Mover el pensamiento de la multitud sobre la plaza es una iniciación en el poder, y hablar para la multitud hasta llevarla a vociferar mi nombre podría ser una forma de la posesión: como si tuviera una mujer debajo de mi cuerpo, justamente poseyéndola, con la sola diferencia que nunca poseer una mujer me trajo un goce comparable.

[Moving the crowd's thoughts over the square is an initiation into power, and speaking to the crowd until I bring it to cry out my name could be a form of possession: as if I had a woman beneath my body, at the very moment of possessing her, with the only difference being that never has possessing a woman brought me a comparable pleasure.]

Marta Lynch[3]

In Pablo Neruda's *Canto general*, the tearful son returns to the lap of his mother, and the virgin continent is violated by North American companies. Octavio Paz organizes his analysis of the Mexican national character in *El laberinto de la soledad* around the taken-for-granted, conflated notions of Indian and female passivity, and domination by means of European, masculine violation. Marta Lynch's protagonist in *La alfombra roja* associates political power with sexual domination, though later he is horrified to see his metaphor made material as he whips the chaotic, malleable, implicitly feminine crowd into such a sexual frenzy that two people actually copulate to his politically seductive words.

Gender difference, particularly as it is played out in heterosexual behavior, is the organizing metaphor in all these texts—poems, essay, novel—and raises the question not of whether gender disparity exists, or even if it helps generate our reality, but of how that fact makes a difference, why it is worth our time to trouble ourselves about it.[4] From the point of view of the dominant group (in this case male), to tamper with gender constructs is to threaten its well-being. The gender-based elite of men (and this is a momentary oversimplification that suppresses other forms of privilege such as class, race, and nationality in order to make a point more clearly) crosses political lines. It is not difficult to understand how conservative forces shore up their ideology with recourse to traditional androcentric notions of womanly obedience and idealization that enclose and exalt womanhood, fetter women's sexuality, and maintain male privilege.[5] But the attachment to gender privilege extends to those men who come from or have expressed solidarity with such disenfranchised groups as workers, peasants, and indigenous people. By rejecting a feminist analysis (and forgetting that half the people in the groups for which they militate are women), they comfortably retain the material advantage of male supremacy (access to women's sexuality, the personal service of wives, mothers, and girlfriends, their twice-sized reflections) while maintaining their radical credentials. Furthermore, reluctance to give up gender privilege on the one hand is matched by hesitancy to accept oneself as an oppressor. If, as traditional Marxism maintains, women are oppressed only by virtue of their class (not gender) position, men as gender are exempt from responsibility for women's oppression.

Undergirding the not-so-simple self-interest in maintaining traditional gender roles and meanings is the naturalization of gender inequality whereby men — and women — of good faith might still believe in the natural or God-given subordination of women to men. This position cannot be supported rationally, but it is a deeply embedded underpinning of Western culture, explained by some theorists as a result of early psychological dynamics in which the mother/father/infant triad results in familiar adult gender relations.[6] These cultural and psychological roots can only be dislodged at a certain psychic expense.

The assumption that women have always been the conservative force in society — counted on not to produce, but to reproduce, to maintain whatever is worth maintaining in the culture — serves masculinist agendas on the left as well as on the right. Women are expected to maintain the home, and they have done so, whether that meant serving as mistress in the enclosure of a big house, going out to the fields to produce the family's food supply, or even traveling many miles to market to sell home-produced goods. For women to venture beyond cultural expectations of familial responsibility, however, in order to look elsewhere — or to look at all — for intellectual and spiritual sustenance is profoundly upsetting to men on the left, who, like those on the right, count on "their" women to maintain, and be, a familiar place of refuge. Where consciousness of exile pervades oppositional sensibility, as it so often does in Latin America, it is women who are invested with the responsibility of representing, and even reproducing, home.

For women to go beyond their boundaries and explore on their own new territory (not the familiar foreign ground of Marx and Engels, or of Derrida and Foucault) is for men not only to lose control of what women think and do, but also for them to lose their link to "home." Deeply embedded in Latin American revolutionary ideology is a longing for a Golden Age, a return to the true culture, tied to indigenous roots, a memory constructed of desire and related to a sort of mythic cultural childhood. The mother at the center of this dream is only partly metaphorical. She is mother country and mother revolution, as in the song by Angel and Isabel Parra, but she is more. The Parras' own mother, Violeta, was a founder, and since her death has become a symbol, of the New Song Movement. She is the mother who seeks out, preserves, and transmits the cultural heritage for "her" children, here in its musical form. In Chile, where Parra worked, the indigenous music she collected and the politically engaged music she wrote were banned as subversive by the Pinochet government, and during his dictatorship her children lived and performed in exile. When Isabel and Angel sing "Madre," their audiences inevitably hear references to Violeta Parra. Without the emotional pull of the real mother, the metaphor of mother would have little power.

The myth of the indigenous mother as the embodiment of racial and cultural heritage, however, masks the more complex relationship between the geopolitical reality of Latin American neocolonialism and a high culture that claims European roots, particularly in the countries whose writers I discuss here. It is probably not a coincidence that the majority of these writers are the daughters or granddaughters of immigrants. Like the United States, much of Latin America has served as a destination for the European (and, to a lesser extent, Asian) diaspora during the nineteenth and twentieth centuries. Poniatowska, Brimmer, Peri Rossi, and Valenzuela all identify strongly as Latin Americans (or as Mexican, Uruguayan, Argentine). Their national identity is not a matter of a racial or essentialist sense of self. It is an identity produced in a particular political and historical crucible, and it crystallized very quickly. Exile from Latin America is not a return to the ancestral home for any of these women; rather, it confirms that the New World is their true home. The North-South distinction is meaningful to these writers because it relies on still another (constructed) power imbalance. A real identification with indigenous

Latin America is possible and encouraged for these women, but their urban background and their access to Western education is an equally valid part of who and what they are. Latin America cannot be the repository of innocence for North American and European women, any more than women can be the reliable home that men can strike out from and return to.[7]

The attention to certain questions of gender equality in traditional socialist writing, and in particular the recognition of the validity of working women's demands for access to employment, equal pay, and political rights in socialist Cuba and Sandinista Nicaragua, has legitimized at least some feminist concerns within the Latin American left. Feminism meets resistance there on the linked issues of foreignness, class allegiance, and sexuality. The mass-media representation of feminism as antisexual and antimale (or, simply and insidiously, antiheterosexual) and the popularly disseminated notion that the feminist movement is bourgeois and Northern (and therefore doubly suspect, probably reactionary) have alienated many otherwise progressive women and men.[8] Women's insistence on controlling their own sexuality, whether in choosing their sexual partners or in having control over reproduction, is represented as anything from perversion to selfishness, and as the work of outside agitators. Despite the fact that for these reasons Latin American textual studies have been slow to legitimate feminism as critical, scholarly practice, it is difficult for a critical analysis of literary texts and social formations to justify ignoring an organizing metaphor as pervasive as gender.[9]

In the first instance feminist theory is about deconstructing the culturally created (but naturalized), bipolar, hierarchical division between male and female in order to understand, and then challenge, the subordinate position of women vis-à-vis men. Once this operation is set in motion, all such divisions are called into question. The first dichotomy feminist theorists understood to be interactive rather than inevitably opposed and separate was that which is sometimes called theory/practice and sometimes mind/body. Feminist work at its richest is always aware of the fundamental connection between these apparent poles. Uprooted from its soil, disengaged from its material sources and consequences, the most brilliant analysis dies. Convenient divisors like race, class, gender, and nationality are not simply separate categories that operate independently if, at times, analogously, but are, rather, interacting phenomena that shade each other's meanings. Similarly, in scholarly analysis, traditional disciplinary boundaries cease to be impermeable as we find that the division of knowledge into categories and of ways of knowing into disciplinary methodologies effectively disallows certain crucial questions and limits the ways to think about answering them if they are so crass as to present themselves anyway. Feminist scholarship in general strives toward interdisciplinarity, so that literary theory and practical criticism are enriched by the work of historians, anthropologists, linguists, philosophers, sociologists, and psychologists. Although we have not escaped disciplinarity, we have begun to look at our own disciplines in the light of others, exposing inadequacies and revealing possibilities.

Like other politically grounded literary criticisms, feminist criticism has gone through its prescriptive stage (i.e., the text *should* denounce gender oppression, or offer positive role models).[10] Traces of this admittedly idealistic and perhaps unsophisticated desire remain in feminist criticism in the intuition that it is important to read women writers because there is a story for us encoded in their texts that careful and clever reading will reveal, because there is a particular set of experiences women record in their texts that speak to other women, because there is a subversion of language that allows us to speak, because there is a tale of oppression, yes, but also of resistance in the very fact that women have claimed the power of the word. Readings of women's writing on these assumptions do not make demands on the content — or even the form — of the text, but first celebrate the very existence of women-authored texts as a testimony to survival, and then scrutinize those texts for strategies that account for that survival. We can applaud some of these strategies, and we might reject others, but we need to learn to recognize all of them.

Although it is not entirely necessary to be a feminist to use the tools of feminist literary analysis, those who engage in the practice are advised to be cognizant of its potential for radical change. By shifting its gaze from men to women, by taking women's lives and their writing seriously, feminist critics crack the bedrock of traditional scholarship. It is not wrong to assume that this collective act may be cataclysmic. No longer can Western man be the norm by which all else is judged. No longer can a simple norm even be posited. With the deconstructionists, feminists have kicked over the box on which Western thought has been standing and calling itself the center. We have not simply moved the center, we are denying its existence. To do so is not to deny reality but to reconnect with it. This is the death of the atomized individual with his disconnected, and thereby objective, view of the world; it is the birth of the relational subject who lives emotionally, spiritually, intellectually, and bodily in connection with and responsible to self and other. It is a utopian goal, perhaps, but also a simple necessity.

In the case of Latin American feminist literary theory (so many qualifiers, marking specificity, enhancing clarity, staking out territory—but also functioning in dynamic relation with other analogously marked forms of feminist analysis), the particular circumstance of each region and the shared history and language of Latin America merit special consideration. Since independence from Spain and Portugal, Latin America has maintained an ideal of continental unity and a history of national sovereignties. Pre-contact indigenous "states" did not conform to what are now the nations of Latin America. And just as it is possible to talk on some level about Latin American literature while on another it makes sense to create divisions by region, or country, or historical era, it is possible to speak in broad terms about a Latin American feminist criticism. This criticism has tended to ally itself with other forms of politically progressive literary analysis, and it shares with them a belief in the relevance of academic critical analysis to social, political, and economic change.

For leftist feminists in Europe, many of whom tend to see all women in developing countries as downtrodden victims, Latin American feminist work can show the resistance and the agency of women—women who are not only the object of the neocolonialist male gaze and the creation of the capitalist patriarchal mind, but also the subjects of their own lives. For the psychoanalytical feminist criticism that returns women's bodies to them for their own pleasure, Latin American feminist criticism offers the reinsertion of that body into the political sphere, which it can, in any case, never truly avoid.

Feminism, like all major political movements today, is both international and local. The availability of books and pamphlets on feminism, the feminist conferences inspired by the galvanizing opening congress in Mexico City of the United Nations Decade for Women, international scholarly meetings, and Pan-American feminist meetings have all contributed to transnational change and growth. At the same time, the local manifestations of feminism, or of women's consciousness of the way gender informs their own lives and the functioning of their own world, and of themselves as political actors, must, by definition, be particular, in response to particular needs. The battered women's shelter in Lima, the communal soup kitchens in the slums of Santiago, and the national campaign against violence against women undertaken by a consortium of Ecuadorian women's groups all mark the growth of a continental feminism.

This movement is separate from, but has ties to, Asian and African feminism as well as to European and North American women's movements. The idealizing tendency toward globalism in feminism (grounded in the belief that all women have something in common) together with a similarly idealized vision of a unified Latin America, allows us to hold the concept of Latin American feminism in our minds, even as we refine the notion with the separate realities not only of different nations and regions in any historical period, but also of power differences of class and race.

One of the conditions of Latin American feminism is that it must be politically progressive and locally motivated. It is clear to me as well that the multiple voices and practices of Latin American feminism (even when it resists that name) must inform the direction of feminist scholarly and theoretical work, just as theory gives coherence to practical feminism. Though its autonomy is crucial, so that it not be tied to or directed by any single political party, feminism in Latin America must look in the same direction as other progressive political movements and work with them in coalition.[11] An outstanding example is the umbrella organization Mujeres por la Vida (Women for Life) in Chile. Under the slogan, "Democracia en el país y en la casa" (Democracy in the nation and in the home), this group united numerous women's organizations, many but not all of them feminist, that saw their feminist goals as bound up with the immediate problem of restoring democracy to a country under dictatorship.

The idea that feminism is a purely European phenomenon developed from Enlightenment theory is, I think, narrow and wrongheaded. It makes more sense to define feminism broadly as the recognition of the systematic inferiorization of women resulting in women's oppression or relative disempowerment, tied to a strategy for changing that circumstance. This definition includes as feminists Spanish women such as Teresa de Cartagena, a fifteenth-century nun whose strategy was not political but theological, and María de Zayas, a seventeenth-century writer, whose concern was limited to the women of the upper classes; and certainly Sor Juana Inés de la Cruz, who defended her right to an intellectual life in seventeenth-century colonial Mexico.

A definition of feminism tied to Enlightenment ideology leads not only to a politically crippling notion of "postfeminism" as Enlightenment thought is increasingly discredited, and to the rejection of feminism as a product of a corrupt and oppressive political philosophy. It also masks forms of feminism developed outside Europe or earlier than the eighteenth century. Women's recognition of their own oppression predates

Rousseau and Mill, and continues into the late twentieth century without showing signs of abating. Feminism cannot be assumed to attach only to the political outgrowths of the Enlightenment, which in fact have legitimated only one version of feminism. Feminism is not static; it takes different forms, and it will be necessary as long as women occupy a subordinate position to men. This notion of the mutability of feminism acknowledges that definitions of men and masculinity, and women and femininity, change. It recognizes that gender relations vary according to time, place, and other categories (race, religion, class, and so on) that attach to individuals in groups. Finally, it acknowledges that feminism itself, as a system of ideas and a strategy for change, is embedded in its particular historical circumstance.

A flexible definition enables feminism to keep revising itself without cutting itself off from its history. Contemporary feminism in the United States is particularly hard on itself: desiring perfection, it is guilt-ridden upon realizing how oppression and subjugation have been carried out, if not in its name, at least with its complicity. However true this may be, feminism's necessary participation in its own time has created this circumstance, and feminists of any one time and place are not to be condemned for neglecting to see all that cultural practice obscures. Yet feminism is also located in no-man's-land, simultaneously outside and inside, which enables it to fashion a critique, however partial, both of itself and of the culture to which it is attached. Therein, precisely, resides its power as a political and theoretical practice.

Feminism is becoming increasingly globalized as it becomes less and less totalizing. Communication technology, the increasing number of international conferences and exchanges between feminist university students and faculty, and international organizations such as the United Nations (whose 1975-85 Decade for Women had profound effects on most nations, if not our own) all make feminism increasingly international. This does not mean a blind acceptance of Western (or, even more limited, U.S.) feminism throughout the world. Rather, with exposure to different forms of feminism, indigenous feminism recognizes itself as such and develops itself from within, borrowing from whatever is useful in foreign feminism and relying on feminist movements internationally to promote their own visibility and legitimation. Not only do indigenous feminist movements refuse to tolerate foreign versions of what feminism ought to look like in their situation (this is especially true when the power relations of the places under consideration are unequal, as they are between the

United States and Latin America), but in fact any feminism imposed from the outside has little chance of survival, since it cannot speak to the needs and concerns of the women on the inside. Feminism must be organic in order to flourish.

While French feminism theorizes alterity and calls it "the feminine," North American feminism creates the "other" out of anything that is not itself. Both strains tend to romanticize the exotic other as well as to foreclose on its potential for resistance to change. The main current of British feminist criticism, with its roots in Marxian analysis, is less academically centered, less formalist, and more overtly political than either French or North American academic criticism, in that it looks at literature as a cultural artifact that mirrors society and which therefore can be analyzed as a manifestation of societal ills. Understandably, it is primarily concerned with British and Commonwealth writing.

The discussion of what feminism means in an international and historical perspective must be broad, and it will no doubt contain inconsistencies and even outright contradictions as it moves through history and from place to place. Sometimes those contradictions will be reconcilable; other times they will not, retaining their unsynthesizable dissimilarities. This is not quite the free play of difference of postmodernism, since these differences are always attached to power, and they remain grounded in material phenomena that are also subject to change.

A blindly middle-class, Europeanized feminism will not do for Latin America, especially when the very models of such a feminism are well into the process of scrutinizing their own class and racial biases. A feminist cultural criticism, of which literary criticism is a part, must take into account not only gender relations but other unequal power relations as well. Because of its Anglocentrism, North American feminist literary theory and criticism, which in its pragmatism, practicality, and commitment to social change has much to offer Latin American criticism, stops at its own borders and only with difficulty sees itself not as normative but as only one mode of being out of many. Similarly, the apparently politically neutral psychoanalytical and semiotic criticism that has been called French feminism is useful only up to a point in creating a Latin American feminist analysis. The emphasis on being embodied, and even "writing the body," can be liberating for women as writers and readers, but what can happen to women's bodies in politically repressive regimes is hardly the *jouissance* Hélène Cixous had in mind. Furthermore, although the notion of language as the internalization of the law of the father that necessarily entraps women is analytically exciting, it is not entirely new to Latin American writers, who have long since known, analogously, that the languages of the colonial powers—Spanish or Portuguese—cannot be used uncritically and that writers are responsible for codifying the new languages that must be forged.

As feminist practice is changing, so must feminism as theoretical construct. For feminist theory is at an impasse. The subject is no longer stable, the "identity" that enables "identity politics" is in question. Experience—what happens to a self in history (and geography)—seems to be representable, even to the individual, only by means of language, itself treacherous insofar as it "means" only by positing lack and difference.[12] The privileged experience of the oppressed is rendered suspect by virtue of the same technologies that it make it legible. Who would say that there is a single woman's experience? Race, class, sexuality, ethnicity, age, religion, geopolitical position—and this is not an exhaustive list—all interact with gender (and each other) to produce experience out of events. If we imagine them as the grid of an intricate plaid we can see women separated from each other, but also woven together into an elaborate pattern. This does not necessarily mean that we are isolated, each of us by her specific configuration, since each of the variables is a locus of identity, which only makes sense in terms of the elements of each configuration and in relation to the pattern as a whole. Some of the relations are, or seem to be, binary oppositions—gender, for example—but others, like ethnicity, are not. Though they may seem to be dichotomous in certain places (Catholic versus Protestant in Northern Ireland, black versus white in North America), such assertions of bipolarity efface the actual multiplicity of positions. There are Jews in Ireland, American Indians and Asians in the United States. Multiple identifiers join us as much as they separate us; some variables are more immediately felt than others (generally speaking, those in which we find ourselves on the oppressed side), and some become important only at certain moments.

Latin American political practice makes available a concept that can get us beyond the subjectivity/identity problem as it is now articulated. Subjectivity can be rescued from solipsism or complete disintegration, and the individual can be redeemed from isolation from others and from representation itself, by the notion of "presence." When victims of repression are honored in Latin America, be they disappeared students or murdered archbishops, their names are called out as if in the rolls, and the collectivity responds "*Presente*," often eliciting the response, "*ahora y para siempre.*" Presence so asserted is at once embodied and represented, individual and historical. It does not rely on a notion of fixity and unchangeability—despite the "now and forever," which is best read as a challenge to death and a promise to continue the struggle against tyranny. The revolutionary project in which "presence" so construed resonates testifies to a belief in radical change, not simply in society but in the relations of individuals as well. "Presence" does not rely on a psychoanalytic explanation of coherence; it is, rather, a notion that posits the sense of self in the quest for transformation. Consciousness-raising is part of this process—it is transformative, collective, and can make for crucial changes in self-definition.[13] This conscious positioning, enabling choice and agency, is what is at stake; not some (as of today) irreconcilable and unanswerable questions about the stability of the psychological subject or the subject as language effect. Presence is created in history and through language; it represents and is represented, but it also acts on material reality.

Presence is claimed in a situation in which some dominant force deliberately denies it.[14] The death of a *compañera* at the hands of a violently repressive government is a vivid example of this. "Presence" is a political claim, which declares the existence of the individual not as a coherent psychological subject, but rather as a potent political subject. Although military discourse provides the term and its context (the soldier present in the ranks), the notion of presence goes beyond militarism or militancy. It is a term that suggests the communal nature of the self—the way in which that fallen, disappeared, invisible one is present in the continued action of others. Otherwise the claim of presence is an empty rhetorical device. The notion of presence can be extended to encompass other sorts of culturally/socially/politically constructed displacements, and it promises to be particularly fruitful in the context of feminist theory. Here I am suggesting that presence—the making visible of the invisible, the continued life of those who have been murdered, the appearance of the disappeared, the testimony that makes whole the body of the tortured—be what we attend to as feminist critics. It is presence in the face of erasure and silencing.

Presence is also associated with scenic interpellation and performance.[15] This kind of presence commands attention. It makes itself known by means of a force expressed as the complex and mysterious combination of a physical and extraphysical attraction, also related to sexuality. Words like "chemistry," "magnetism," and "charisma" are commonly associated with it. There is an intentionality and artifice about this sort of presence as well—think of "stage presence." The performative and aesthetic aspects of presence in this guise, its interactive quality, and its connection to sexuality, all add to the usefulness of "presence" as a concept around which to crystallize a theory of politics and sexuality for the study of literary texts.

Most compelling about the trope of presence for Latin American feminist literary analysis is its inexorably political tone. If feminism is to function as a form of analysis and as a tool for social change, it must address the needs of the society in which it occurs. As a progressive political stance, feminism cannot be separate from other struggles for liberation and equality. And while all these struggles are, arguably, interconnected, they have quite different manifestations from country to country, region to region. In Latin America feminism is by necessity intertwined with other progressive political movements. Its inevitable arguments with those movements need to take place within a spirit of solidarity and often require concessions to immediate needs that can make North American feminists impatient. On the other hand, Latin American feminism retains a revolutionary edge and a belief in the efficacy of political intervention that, in academic feminism at least, seem to be waning in the United States. Connected as it is to a progressive, usually leftist, political program, Latin American feminism does not see itself as eternally oppositional. It struggles toward change, confident that change can occur. Euramerican theoretical feminism, particularly in its psychoanalytic mode, has become too comfortable with the subordination of "the feminine," and its use as an almost mathematical constant to represent "difference" or "otherness," without much reflecting on the implications of this theorizing for living women. Among North American varieties of feminism, Latin American feminism undoubtedly comes closest to black and Latina feminism in its political and economic urgency, its multiple allegiances, and its questioning of the effects of universalizing the notion of woman when that universalizing occurs from a dominant position.[16]

Presence suggests more than simple visibility, an early goal of Anglo-American feminist work. It includes the reader's recognition of the text as a form of practice, connected to existing ideological formations in a combination of resistance and complicity; and it is a reminder of the responsibility that we as readers, critics, and political actors have in addressing these texts.

3

The Presence in Absence of Exile

Que lo sepan todos de una vez: el exilio no puede más ser una retórica.
Cristina Peri Rossi[1]

To get to the presence of women writers in Latin America we must traverse the terrain of its apparent opposite. It is in their absence that women have loomed in traditional accounts of the region's literature. The inclusion of a handful of them in the official histories underscores each one's apparent exceptionality. For the few whose writing is widely acknowledged, as well as for those whose names are rarely mentioned, absence is a complex and burdened notion. It is a Pandora's box of meaning, containing silence and invisibility, censorship and self-censorship, disappearance and exile.

The psychoanalytic school that is often called French feminism posits "the feminine" as a lack and "woman" as an empty space, a grammatical marker that makes the presence of the masculine possible. In this account "feminine" is not the separate-but-equal counterpart of "masculine," but the embodiment (if such a thing can be possible) of absence itself.[2] The trope of woman-as-absence naturalizes women's own absence from literary history and conceals the material practices that account for the lack of women's names in the literary canon. It tends to make the existence of embodied women beside the point and renders women's own absence a nonissue. In so doing, it traps the woman writer in an untenable situation, where she cannot be fully absorbed into phallic presence—that which is visible, takes space, enters, asserts, demands. Nor, as the usurper of language, can she be relegated to vaginal silence, dark, emptiness, the no-place that the masculine intrudes upon to make his presence meaningful. The woman writer is consigned to anomaly, accounted for by means of the sort of gender acrobatics that enabled nineteenth-century commentators to declare of the prolific Gertrudis Gómez de Avellaneda, "That woman is some man!"

Woman-as-absence may seem a short step from women's absence, but the phrases are radically different from one another. "Woman" (as absence) is exactly analogous to zero, the place marker empty in and of itself, but crucial for any complex calculation. Women, plural, fill time and space; the possessive implies a subject position. "Women's absence" is a conundrum implying a presence elsewhere. This is the hope nestled in the dark bottom of the Pandora's box of "absence": the hidden obverse, unacknowledged presence.

Women have, in fact, been writing since the earliest days of colonization. One of the chronicles, those reports written by explorers, conquistadors, and settlers that are the earliest manifestations of Latin American literature, was written by Isabel de Guevara in 1556.[3] Some of her contemporaries, mostly wives and daughters of colonial government functionaries, wrote poetry, anticipating the key figure of Spanish American colonial letters. Sor Juana Inés de la Cruz who wrote learned treatises, poetry, and plays in the seventeenth century, strongly defended women's right to live a full intellectual life. Although she was far from being the only woman writer of her day, the brightness of Sor Juana's star has blinded most literary historians to other suns.[4] In the 1800s Juana Manuela Gorriti wrote political novels in Argentina, and Gertrudis Gómez de Avellaneda, well known for her poetry, plays, fiction, and essays, wrote *Sab,* the first antislavery novel in the Americas. Later in the century Clorinda Matto de Turner published *Aves sin nido (Birds without Nests),* becoming the first writer in the Americas to use the novel to confront the oppression of the indigenous peoples. The nineteenth century also saw the rise of literary salons in Peru, where groups of women writers, including Gorriti and Matto de Turner, met regularly to read and discuss their work.

In the first part of the twentieth century the rise of feminism and a modest increase in literacy in much of Latin America was accompanied by increasing numbers of women writers: the poets Julia de Burgos in Puerto Rico, Delmira Agustini and Juana de Ibarbourou in Uruguay, and Alfonsina Storni in Argentina; and novelists Norah Lange in Argentina,

María Luisa Bombal in Chile, Teresa de la Parra in Venezuela. In 1945, the first Nobel Prize in literature to be won by a Latin American went to the Chilean poet Gabriela Mistral. In the fifties and sixties, Rosario Castellanos (Mexico), Marta Lynch, Silvina Bullrich, and Beatriz Guido (Argentina), Clarice Lispector (Brazil), Marta Traba (Argentina), Elena Garro (Mexico), and Marta Brunet and Mercedes Valdivieso (Chile) were active writers, yet the story of the "Boom" of Latin American literature does not mention these names, nor do accounts of post-Boom literature of the seventies and eighties regularly name their successors, among them Isabel Allende (Chile), Luisa Valenzuela (Argentina), Julieta Campos and Margo Glantz (Mexico), Nélida Piñón (Brazil), Rosario Ferré and Ana Lydia Vega (Puerto Rico), Albalucía Angel (Colombia), Elvira Orphée (Argentina), Gioconda Belli (Nicaragua).[5] Although absence from official accounts does not mean nonexistence, "woman writer" remains a fugitive category in Latin American literature.

Exile is a particular form of presence-in-absence whose complex play of apparent opposites marks an intersection of Latin American and feminine experience, not least because, although both conditions are considered deviant, exile and femininity both occur with striking frequency, often in the same place. As writers, women and exiles have both been rendered invisible, though in different ways. Women's literary history has been annulled in Latin America, making the occasional woman writer named in conventional literary history appear to be exceptional. On the other hand, many male writers have become widely known, but the fact of their exile has not. Angel Rama's observation that "literary production in forced or voluntary exile is almost a continental standard from Alaska to Tierra del Fuego" was not really news, but stated that way it astonished nonetheless, for the way it made us rethink the meaning of "American" literature.[6] Even when the idea of women writers becomes plausible, the possibility of thinking about them as exile writers is hampered by the association of women with "home." The preceding chapter's opening quotations from Paz and Neruda settle women into permanence and passivity. Women were present when the foreign adventurers arrived from Spain, and they remained as motherland itself when their sons went into exile. The trope of the earthbound mother is a potent literary figure, but it is hardly a complete representation of material reality. Women leave home, too. Poor women move in vast numbers from the countryside to the cities, and from one country to another, in search of economic survival. The cruelly named low-intensity warfare aimed primarily at rural civilian populations that has so badly harmed so much of Central America in the past years has created masses of refugees, many of whom are women; the military coups of the early 1970s in Chile, Argentina, and Uruguay sent many women into exile.

Whether forced or voluntary, exile is primarily from, and not to, a place. It thus carries something of the place departed and of the historical circumstance of that place at the moment of departure, making the exiled person no longer present in the place departed, but not a part of the new place either.[7] In naming herself an expatriate, Luisa Valenzuela still describes the state of suspension I am calling exile:

> My Argentine society does not exist anymore; in many ways it is ended.
> I am not an exile; I am an expatriate in the sense that I do not have any
> homeland anymore. They have managed to kill our country in a variety
> of ways, so it is a very painful situation to deal with, but at the same
> time it is a reality one cannot deny. So even if I went back to my
> country, which I could, being quite careful, it would not be the same
> place I used to love.[8]

Language tells us that exile is its own location: people living out of their homeland are "*in* exile." It is not surprising that the physical place of exile is often perceived as a noncountry, not as a different one. The place of exile is defined by what is missing, not by what it contains. Gabriela Mistral's "País de la ausencia" ("Land of Absence"), written when she was living in Provence, evokes such a place.[9] It is weightless and empty and cannot sustain her:

> País de la ausencia,
> extraño país,
> más ligero que ángel
> y seña sutil . . .
> No echa granada
> no cría jazmín,
> y no tiene cielos
> ni mares de añil.
> Nombre suyo, nombre,
> nunca se lo oí
>
> [Land of absence,
> strange land,

lighter than angel
or subtle sign . . .
It bears no pomegranate
nor grows jasmine,
and has no skies
or indigo seas.
Its name, a name
that has never been heard]

This shadow land stands in sharp contrast to the place departed, which is
dense and full of color and provides the restoration of sleep and nourish-
ment:

Perdí cordilleras
en donde dormí;
perdí huertos de oro
dulces de vivir;
perdí yo las islas
de caña y añil,
y las sombras de ellos
me las vi ceñir
y juntas y amantes
hacerse país.

[I lost ranges of mountains
wherein I could sleep.
I lost orchards of gold
that were sweet to live.
I lost islands of indigo
and sugar cane,
and the shadows of these
I saw circling me,
and together and loving
became a land.][10]

The sense of loss in exile that informs this poem is also palpable in

"The Emigrant Jew," in which a Jewish woman in exile during the Second World War speaks of being "cut off from the earth" (Mistral, 135). In "The Foreigner," the speaker observes the unalterable alienation of the foreign woman who lives in her town, and in "The Disburdened," the exile's sense of emptiness becomes a metaphor for death.

Longing, nostalgia, a wish to return and a fear of returning, are all marks of exile. Furthermore, the political exile, who is both outcast and survivor, has a complex relationship with those who remain in the homeland. Feelings of guilt both for having survived and for having abandoned others, mixed with a sense of responsibility for keeping the culture alive and the struggle against oppression ongoing, can coexist with a desire to forget and rest. Exile is dislocation, both physical and psychic. The exile is the stranger, not seen, misperceived. The departure into absence of exile contains and fosters a will to return into presence. The exile's writing aims to win back the land; its longed-for destination is that one place where it can no longer be.[11]

The exile is the quintessential foreigner, unknown and unknowable. In Cristina Peri Rossi's "La ciudad" (The city) even the experience of alienation is denied to the exile by acquaintances who believe that he has had plenty of time to acculturate. Peri Rossi's striking imagery evoking the sense of loss in exile is reminiscent of Mistral's.[12] In "Las estatuas, o la condición del extranjero" (Statues, or the foreigner's condition), the country of exile is represented by the town square. Though it is the center of community for those who have always lived there, the square is recognizable to the foreigner only by its shape. All the human and social institutions that ordinarily frame and define it—church, houses, even jail—are absent. Nature barely survives. This null space, first described as empty, is in fact densely populated with lifeless, immobile people, who, to the narrator, seem to be statues. They do not see him, do not admit him into what for them must be life but for him has none of the warmth and color of life. (The morning on which the story takes place is icy, and one statue that catches his eye has a white body and an absent look.) The foreigner is simply unseen. His sense of causing disturbance is deflected inward since the statues cannot be aware of it; the only one disturbed is himself:

> Nadie me miraba, pero era aquella ausencia de contemplación precisamente lo que me hacía sentir extraño. Descubrí, entonces, que la condición del extranjero es el vacío: no ser reconocido por los que ocupan un lugar por el solo derecho de estar ocupándolo. (132)

[No one looked at me, but it was precisely that absence of
contemplation that made me feel strange. I discovered then that the
foreigner's condition is the void: not to be recognized by those who
occupy a place simply because they are there.][13]

Rendered invisible by those around him, the speaker projects his own
emptiness onto his surroundings. Here, as in Mistral, the familiar items
of home are displaced but not replaced, and the land of exile becomes a
spectral land of absence.

Even if psychologically painful, it is politically expedient for the land
of exile to be an unreal place. Luis, Vázquez, and Ali, the exile leaders of
Marta Traba's posthumous novel *En cualquier lugar* (Anywhere), con-
sciously maintain their status as outsiders, organizing a squatters' village
in the railway station, a place of transit.[14] They actively disapprove of
those of their compatriots who attempt to integrate themselves into their
adoptive country, since those who do so must refocus their energy away
from political strategizing and action directed toward the lost homeland.
Moreover, willingness to adapt to the new may be a form of accepting
defeat, of acknowledging that it may never be possible to go home again.

Exile writing is a discourse of desire, a desire to recuperate, repair, and
return.[15] This apparently conservative desire rests, however, on a project
of transformation. Not only is return to the homeland in its present condition insufficient; for the political exile it is impossible. Exile writers are
bound to the parent culture in an effort to criticize and recreate it, within
the framework of a potentially liberatory international culture. Not immediately constrained by the cultural norms of their adopted lands, exile
writers are freed into a perspective of universality from which to contem-
plate their now-distant homes.[16] Their writing, as a result, is both accessible and exotic to an international public, partaking as it does of international norms in the service of a particular history, culture, and
tradition. This in part accounts for the international interest in Latin
American writing since the 1960s. Another factor, also related to the phenomenon of exile, is the proximity of the writers themselves to the international market. It is not surprising that the majority of Latin American
writers who are best known internationally are those who live, or have
lived, abroad. This freedom, however, has its price: a sense of dislocation.[17]

Not only the place of exile, but the homeland as well, is a dream space
to the exile. The final third of Luisa Valenzuela's novel *Como en la*

guerra, the part that takes place on the American continent, may be a dream.[18] Valenzuela is deliberately ambiguous in her depiction of the distorted landscapes of America that might be the effects of peyote and political repression, or simply the continent as dreamscape.[19] At the end of part 2, the protagonist is about to set sail for America. On the dock he falls asleep and dreams his return. Whether or not he wakes up and boards the ship before he is found in Mexico at the beginning of part 3 is never resolved.

Cristina Peri Rossi's "La ciudad," included in the collection *El museo de los esfuerzos inútiles*, contains an exile's recurrent dream of the native city he left sixteen years before. In a classic example of the uncanny, his dream combines reassuringly familiar details—a courtyard filled with flowers and mosaic, the window of a friend's house—with disconcerting ones—spinning mountains, trees with blue leaves, an empty urban landscape, and an enigmatic presence that most disturbs the protagonist because he cannot ascertain its gender. As a result the protagonist feels that he both does and does not belong to the city. Caught between home and exile, desire and fear, followed by an ambiguously gendered presence that is oppressive and annihilating, the protagonist is consigned to, and consumed by, his nightmare city.

Another dream text by Peri Rossi, contained in a poem from a collection called *Estado de exilio* (State of exile), drives the speaker to ask if the home city ever even existed:

> Soñé que me iba lejos de aquí
> el mar estaba picado
> olas negras y blancas
> un lobo muerto en la playa
> un madero navegando
> llamas en altamar.
>
> ¿existió alguna vez una ciudad llamada Montevideo?
>
>
> [I dreamed I was going far from here
> the sea was choppy
> black and white waves
> a dead wolf on the beach

a wooden plank sailing
through flames on the open sea.

did there ever exist a city called Montevideo?][20]

Peri Rossi's images of death and loss are echoed in Valenzuela's *Como en la guerra*, where the return to the home city also ends in destruction. Valenzuela's protagonist, AZ, goes back to Buenos Aires in a progressive, almost linear movement toward the destruction of the center of power. A group of old Indian women in rural Mexico begins to reinitiate AZ into America. His guide, the spirit of his former lover, *la otra*, is slowly revealed to him.[21] He comes to know her true name and something of her experience in America. She is finally revealed to him in the end, apotheosized into the liberated spirit of America ascending heavenward in the wake of the explosion that destroys the locus of oppression.

Perhaps the most comprehensive image of the departed homeland is *la otra's* stream-of-consciousness description of the "house" she was obliged to leave. Inside, the house appears to be made up of a series of long stone corridors, all leading to a capricious clock, behind which is a narrow, heavy wooden door. The house is the site of a contest, and whoever loses must leave. The mechanical clock, a cruel parody of a heart, coldly decides the contest.

From the outside, the house is an impregnable cement cube. What seemed long and narrow from within now "debe de haber mil cuartos clausurados, habitaciones secretas en grandes cantidades . . . donde quizá esté la verdad que buscamos, donde quizá se encierre la luz que está en la mente de todos aunque nadie la nombre" (69) [(appears) to have a thousand closed-off rooms, secret rooms in great quantities . . . where perhaps lies the truth we seek, where perhaps the light that is in the minds of all of us is enclosed, though no one mentions it]. Once outside, the speaker understands that it is not daylight they are seeking, but rather "other levels of reality" (69; my translation).

This metaphor describes the conundrum of the political exile. Inside the repressive system all pressure is exerted to prevent protest or rebellion. The clock has a viper in its belly, and the menace of the narrow door is reiterated by the many cruciform doors, suggesting martyrdom, throughout the house. Once the narrator has entered the contest, played, and lost, she must leave, for she has heard that unspeakable things happen to those who lose and remain. Banished, she circles the house and discovers its real shape, but she cannot get this information to those still inside, any more than they can speak to her. Only by leaving could she learn the other shape of the house and that the truth, its hope, comes from within.

Neither the knowledge gained from within the house (immersion in one's own culture) nor that gained from without (the internationalist perspective) is sufficient by itself. The exile, however, cannot have both at the same time.[22] The exile can never be sufficiently present anywhere.

The exiled figures of Mistral's poems are women, but both Peri Rossi and Valenzuela choose men as their exiled protagonists in the texts considered here. Yet for these male characters the experience of exile is the experience of being feminized, for the condition of exile and the condition of women in patriarchal culture are remarkably alike. Experiences familiar to women—of being invisible, of having their reality misinterpreted by the dominant group, of being marginalized, of having unwanted characteristics displaced onto them—are undergone by AZ and Peri Rossi's exiles. In "La ciudad" the protagonist's ex-wife

> experimentaba un fuerte sentimiento de rechazo por cualquier país no europeo, convencida, de manera oscura e incontrolable, de que más allá del océano comenzaba un mundo diverso, lleno de pestes malignas, comidas envenenadas, criaturas esperpénticas, animales salvajes, volcanes coléricos, ríos que se precipitan y una suciedad general. Las largas conversaciones que él había tenido, para convencerla de que las cosas *no eran exactamente así*, chocaban con una resistencia que mucho más que racional era instintiva: como si Luisa quisiera defenderse de un peligro muy grande, que había colocado más allá del océano, para poder vivir cómodamente y en paz de este otro lado. (167; emphasis in the original)

> [experienced a strong feeling or rejection toward any non-European country, convinced in an obscure and uncontrollable way that beyond the ocean a different world began, filled with malignant disease, poisoned food, grotesque creatures, wild animals, choleric volcanoes, raging rivers, and a general dirtiness. The long conversations that he had had to convince her that things *weren't exactly like that* clashed with a resistance that much more than rational was instinctive: as if Luisa wanted to defend herself against a great danger, which she had placed across the ocean, in order to live comfortably and in peace on this other side.]

This is not to say that the protagonists of "La cuidad" and *Como en la guerra* cease to behave in traditionally masculinist ways. AZ asserts his participation in European high culture with some ferocity. He is a semi-otician at the University of Barcelona, hiding behind the distanced "we" of scholarly discourse in his study of a prostitute. At the same time, however, he longs to return to Argentina, to drink familiar wine and eat familiar food. AZ's self-delusion is such that not only does he fail to see that the individual whose essence he is searching for is himself; he also believes that he is analyzing *la otra* rather than constructing her out of his own needs. He slowly comes to understand that he is trying to find himself through her, that as an Argentine she somehow represents his past. *La otra* is, however, unwilling to talk about her past and thus refuses AZ access to the Argentina of what he assumes to be their mutual memories. When *la otra* finally disappears, leaving no hope for him to return figuratively through her, he decides to make the actual journey back. Like Peri Rossi's character in "La ciudad," AZ sees the possibility of reintegration of the self in the return to his native land. The male exile in these texts is lost, confused, alienated, and in search of himself via a reconciliation with his past and a connection with the feminine. (The protagonist's guide in "La ciudad" may or may not be a woman, but the very mystery of its gender suggests femininity.) This is a familiar pattern of desire, yet exile offers other possibilities: the discovery within the self of a capacity to survive and grow in the new environment, and transcendence, realized in Peri Rossi and Valenzuela by women.

The only figure to be strengthened by the disaster in Peri Rossi's *Descripción de un naufragio* (Description of a shipwreck) is a woman.[23] The shipwreck serves as a metaphor for the military takeover of Uruguay, the sailors are political activists who are advised by their captain to save themselves at the moment it becomes clear that their cause is lost, and one woman, observed by her husband and the captain, follows that advice. Three of the four poems concerning her escape into exile are spoken by the husband, who is surprised to discover that she is strong, brave, and magnificent in her decisiveness, as well as selfish and despicable for abandoning him and their comrades. The fourth poem (actually the third in the series, allowing the man to have the last word) is spoken by the woman, who discovers that the catastrophe has given her the opportunity to act for herself, to survive, to be, in fact, reborn. What seems coldness and strength to her husband (her not looking back as she rows away) is, for her, an admission of sentiment. The woman reports that only by suppressing the desire to look back could she be sure of her ability to escape and survive (81-90).

Once she has taken the courageous leap into an unknowable future, the woman finds the physical strength to save herself. Survival, however, must constantly be won, and in other texts by Peri Rossi it is again the female character who has the competence to survive. Alicia, the child in "La influencia de Edgar Allan Poe en la poesía de Raimundo Arias" (The influence of Edgar Allan Poe on the poetry of Raimundo Arias), a story included in *La tarde del dinosaurio,* assumes the role of parent when she and her father are in exile in Spain. In the improbable disguise of a South American Indian (the European confusion about the meaning of Latin America enables her to carry off the masquerade), she begs enough money for them to live. Her father, at a loss in Europe like the other male exiles in these stories, is politically, economically, and socially impotent.[24]

In Traba's *En cualquier lugar,* the men seem to believe that their political strategizing and their insistence on remaining outsiders are effective and useful, but the widowed Alicia is impatient to get on with her life. Mariana is both angry *and* impatient at what she perceives to be the men's self-importance and their romanticizing of exile. Like Peri Rossi's little girl, she finds them ultimately ineffectual.

In Peri Rossi's and Traba's texts both male and female exile characters remain recognizable representations of ordinary human beings caught in painful social, political, and spiritual circumstances. In Valenzuela, on the other hand, the female exile is empowered with extrahuman capacities. In her depiction of *la otra,* Valenzuela taps into potent myths of female transcendence and regeneration. Though to a certain extent it is AZ's overwrought imagination that construes *la otra* as a magical being, the reader is left enough freedom in this ambiguous text to accept such a reading of the character.

La otra exemplifies what Nina Auerbach calls the "angelic demon who becomes the source of all shaping and creative power . . . as she forecasts apocalyptic new orders" (188). She is "not a human but a magnetic object, the angelic power that generates and orders the novel's vital world" (88).[25] On the simplest level of plot, *la otra* determines AZ's movements: his nighttime forays to meet her, his decision to return to America, his participation in the resistance. Formally, the novel mimics her manner of thinking, combining the affective with the intellectual, embracing ambiguity, blurring traditional notions of time and space. That *la otra* is a writer is not at all incidental. Her scribbled and forgotten messages are part of the text that AZ struggles to interpret.[26] His failure to do so is caused in large part by his incomprehension of her will—to say nothing of her ability—to transcend common reality and of her concomitant decision never to look back.

La otra's refusal to acknowledge AZ as someone she knew in Buenos Aires, her more general silence concerning her past, her easy participation in both the prostitutes' milieu and AZ's high-powered intellectual analysis, her constant and seemingly effortless moves from country to country, her transforming masks and costumes, and her guiltless sexuality, all mark the character as demonic in Auerbach's terms:

> The female demonic knows no social boundaries and no fond regrets. Instead, in its purest form it is animated by a longing not for childhood but for transcendence. (104)

While AZ longs for home, for a return to the place of childhood, *la otra* wants only to move on.

The rupture that causes anguish in the male exile originates in the vital connection between the citizen (by definition male) and his country, which is severed in the condition of exile.[27] Integrity for the male exile is possible only if he returns home, or if, as in *En cualquier lugar,* he reproduces "home" in the place of exile. AZ's alienated "we" at the beginning of the novel becomes the problematic "I/he" as he acknowledges his alienation en route home, and is finally resolved in the integrated "I" with his return to Argentina and political action. The female exile, who was never completely at one with her country, experiences a different sort of split. It would be both cruel and naive to suggest that women do not suffer in exile, but they may also have something particular to gain from exile as women, free of the oppressive sexism of the home culture. The rupture a woman experiences is not a rending from an always-nourishing home, but a mitosis, a split not from but within the self, into two distinct beings—the self and the double—that can enable transcendence.

The means by which transcendence is sought through the double is different in each of these writers. In Mistral's "Emigrada judía" ("The Emigrant Jew") the division into self and other is imposed by the circumstances of the speaker's flight:

> Una soy a mis espaldas,
> otra volteada al mar:
> mi nuca hierve de adioses,
> y mi pecho de ansiedad. (134)

[I am one at my back,
another turned to the sea:
The nape of my neck seethes with goodbyes,
and my breast with yearning. (135)]

The one that looks back is ultimately shed, leaving only the self that faces
the future:

¡y aventada mi memoria
llegaré desnuda al mar! (136)

[With memory blown clean by the wind,
I arrive naked at the sea. (137)]

This survival into a new future is achieved only at great loss. The past is
wrenched from the speaker and she has no choice but to accept its disappearance as a condition of her survival.[28]

Sadness and loss also accompany *la otra's* transcendence and survival
in *Como en la guerra,* but unlike Mistral's Holocaust survivor, Valenzuela's character makes a conscious decision to abandon her double. In this
case the double is a twin sister who, until the moment of *la otra's* exile,
lived the same political life as she. *La otra's* reticence with AZ, whom she
suspects of being a CIA agent, is due primarily to her desire to protect her
twin, whom she left behind and who is still involved in the resistance. Far
from forgetting her, *la otra* cherishes this other self, even though it was
necessary to leave her.[29]

In Peri Rossi's *Lingüística general,* the speaker achieves transcendence
by embracing the double, who in this case originates outside the self. She
is the speaker's lover, who reflects, confirms, and enlarges her reality. An
early poem in the collection specifically connects the damaging experience of political exile to the healing encounter with the beloved. In this
poem, the nightmare image of blue-leaved trees, which haunted the protagonist of "La ciudad," becomes a symbol of transformation, a promise
of hope and love.

The final section of *Lingüística general* chronicles the travels of the
lovers through Europe. Now, movement from place to place is wholly
voluntary and joyful. The lovers, as lesbians, know that they can never
belong to the places they visit, nor do they have any desire to. Yet they are
far from invisible, taking a playful pleasure from

escandalizando a los peces
y a los buenos ciudadanos de éste (74)

[scandalizing the fish and
the good citizens]

For the speaker, the lover is "mi semejante mi igual mi parecida" (my double, my equal, my likeness) and "mi hermana" (my sister) (74). They share identities by wearing each other's clothes and by claiming as their own the other's body and history:

Te amo esta y otras noches
con las señas de identidad
cambiadas
como alegremente cambiamos nuestras ropas
y tu vestido es el mío
y mis sandalias son las tuyas
Como mi seno
es tu seno
y tus antepasadas son las mías (74)

[I love you this and other nights
with our signs of identity
exchanged
as joyfully we switch clothes
and your dress is mine
and my sandals are yours
As my breast
is your breast
and your ancient mothers are my own]

This personal transcendence is not achieved at the expense of political consciousness and action. The speaker knows that the relationship between them is a "subversión al orden domesticado" (subversion of the domestic order) (74). *Lingüística general*, written several years after Peri Rossi's initial exile, comes to terms with new life in Europe. In "Te conocí en septiembre" (I met you in September), exile becomes rebirth:

Te conocí en septiembre
y era otoño en el hemisferio de los grandes
            fósiles marinos,
y era primavera en el país cuya guerra perdimos
—bellos e ingenuos como niños—
y violento nos despidió
cuyas heridas llamamos
segundo nacimiento, exilio
            —meditación amarga o desengaño—

[I met you in September
and it was autumn in the hemisphere
            of the great marine fossils,
and it was spring in the country whose war we had lost
—beautiful and naive as children—
and violently it sent us off
whose wounds we call
second birth, exile
            —bitter meditation or disillusionment]

Mistral's emigrant Jew, Valenzuela's *la otra*, Peri Rossi's speaker, and Traba's Alicia all turn toward the new world that exile offers them. These figures participate in a liberating, boundaryless culture. As embodiments of female transcendence, they most clearly fulfill the promise of exile as a means to deeper levels of understanding and the broad perspective that Angel Rama describes (17).

One result of this wider perspective is a more acute consciousness of language. Peri Rossi lives in Spain, where her language was codified and where no little snobbery about the purity of the language can be found, but she lives in the region of Catalonia, where language is a highly politicized issue.[30] Luisa Valenzuela resided for many years in New York City, where her native language was, ambiguously, both a foreign tongue and a low-status domestic language.

For the exile writer, language is the means by which the connection with a fragmented culture can be maintained. But just as the view of one's country changes with the move from inside to outside, the sound of one's language takes on new tones when it is heard at a distance. Pedro Orgambide tells how hearing Spanish spoken in his new country calls into play feelings of foreignness, belonging, nostalgia, and identity, all at once.[31] The dislocation produced by exile serves to clarify and intensify linguistic identity.[32] In Traba's novel some exiles cite political purity to justify their refusal to learn the language of the country that has offered them refuge, yet they become dependent on those who, for expediency's sake, do learn.

Given the emotional cargo that language bears for the exile and the professional stake that the writer has in it, it is not surprising that writers like Peri Rossi and Valenzuela make language a primary theme in their work. Both writers are relentlessly modern, maintain thick narrative masks, and rupture traditional narrative patterns. Their writing requires constant work on the part of the reader. Peri Rossi asks not for the suspension of disbelief of anecdotal fiction, since her stories often have no plot, but rather for a submission to emotive states. Valenzuela conserves the elements of traditional fiction—time, space, character, action—but she confounds the mixture in an apparently haphazard form. Given all the elements of a fiction, the reader tries to (re)construct the anecdote. Ironically, despite the fact that AZ must learn that the story he wants to read is his own, the reader soon learns that *la otra*'s story is most compelling. In Valenzuela the suppression of the anecdote is apparent rather than real, and the question of just which anecdote is primary remains unresolved.

Peri Rossi does not altogether eschew anecdote, but she tends to locate it in her lyric poetry. If Valenzuela questions generic paradigms from within, by confusing the terms of the novel form inside the novel itself, Peri Rossi questions them externally, by reassigning narrative function from the story to the poem and by using the story form to evoke states of consciousness and emotion.

This formal experimentation escapes being a series of sterile language games because of the political reality against the shadow of which these texts flash light. Exile is real or imminent for these writers, and it intrudes as lived reality in their work. Peri Rossi ends *Descripción de un naufragio* with a list of names of people who died as a result of the military coup in Uruguay, and she refers her readers to newspapers for further details, thus casting the entire book of poetry as testimony.

Marta Traba's formal experimentation is most pronounced in such earlier texts as *Homérica latina*, and even *Los laberintos insolados*. In her last novels, *Conversación al sur (Mothers and Shadows)*, and *En cualquier lugar*, she seems to be returning to a simpler, more traditional and accessible narrative that communicates as much as it represents.[33] Language is a refuge, as one of Peri Rossi's few women protagonists claims in "Las avenidas de la lengua" (*El museo de los esfuerzos inútiles*), because it is a connective device, and not only because it can conceal and protect even as it reveals. The narrator of the final story in Valenzuela's *Aquí pasan cosas raras (Strange Things Happen Here)* lives in internal exile. She longs for the day when she can come out of hiding, find the texts she knows her countrymen and women are writing, and begin to write in the first person feminine. As things are, all those freedoms are too dangerous to risk; for the time being, the writing must remain hidden and the identity of the writer must remain secret. But the texts are there, waiting for the right time to assert their presence. Choosing the wrong time can be fatal. In *Conversación al sur*, Dolores — the child of the younger generation — returns from prison only to be captured again, this time taking with her the older generation's Irene, who had until then been safe. The protagonist of Valenzuela's allegory *Realidad nacional desde la cama* (National reality from bed), undergoes the paralyzing experience of returning to her homeland after democracy has ostensibly been restored, and finding the culture stripped.[34] The economy is a meaningless, if deadly, joke; reality is willfully distorted, represented only indirectly, on a television screen. The maid, who is there to "clean up," "keep things in order," and "keep an eye on" the protagonist (all these tasks to be multiply understood), struggles to keep the protagonist from witnessing the national crisis. The country is reconstructed as country club, hedged in on one side by ever-growing numbers of the poor and dispossessed, and on the other by an unrepentant and power-hungry military. Having returned either too soon or too late, the protagonist is virtually silenced and finds herself unable to act.

That "right time" for return must be determined by political action. In *Como en la guerra* (an earlier text, written when solutions that were either pragmatic or nonviolent seemed unlikely) the journey to America begins as a search for self through sex, ritual, hallucination, animism, and Christianity. Yet in this text, which refuses to resolve the ambiguity between the phenomenal and the imagined, which asserts that the fictionality of the work claims the right and even the inevitability of ambiguity, the quest is resolved on the material level. In a sudden break with his journey to spiritual transcendence via love, death, and ritual, AZ realizes that personal salvation means nothing in the face of material suffering:

> Y él decide sobre la poca importancia que tiene el llegar a la cumbre, el llevar una máscara y el amor o la muerte frente a los problemas verdaderos del hombre: el hambre y la ignominia.
>
> Corre entonces camino abajo, se sacude la máscara, se aleja en una lancha a motor y se interna en el monte donde sabe que andan sus hermanos. (161)
>
> [And he makes a decision about the unimportance of reaching the peak, wearing a mask and love or death, in contrast to man's real problems: hunger and ignominy.
>
> Then he runs downward, he rips off the mask, he rides away in a motorboat and he enters the backlands where he knows his brothers and sisters are.]

La otra's secret name is then revealed to him. The name is his key to salvation not because it gives him access to some supernatural gift, but because it opens his way to political action. Knowledge of *la otra*'s nom de guerre gives AZ entry into the guerrilla. He comes to know her by taking on the political work she abandoned.

AZ's rebirth into the guerrilla counterweighs *la otra*'s death of hope, a death that in a curious way disembodies her. Having lost "the life when she had consciousness of things and she struggled for a concrete cause and felt sure of herself," she becomes incorporeal. She never seems to buy food or eat, and she can apparently travel through time and space without recourse to modern means of transportation. Paradoxically, her alienation takes a peculiarly female and embodied form: she becomes a prostitute. (Valenzuela is not content to leave *la otra* with no political work, however. She earns the anger of the neighborhood by organizing the prostitutes for better pay and working conditions.) Suspended somewhere between all-body and no-body, in exile *la otra* becomes a symbol of degradation and of the transcendence AZ thought he was seeking. In fact, *la otra*'s true moment of sublimity was previous to her exile, during the time she integrated body and spirit in the struggle for her country's liberation:

> En la selva las historias escondidas afloran como el vaho desde el fondo mismo de la putrefacción de las hojas, pero la putrefacción no las alcanza. Eso ocurre con ella, o con el recuerdo de ella en la selva, que se agranda como fue grande en una época que él ignora pero intuye. Ella, la prostituta, fue sublime entonces y él tiene que saberlo de alguna

manera, no puede ser que haya gastado y gaste tanto esfuerzo para simplemente compenetrarse de una alma femenina. (163)

[In the jungle hidden stories flower like vapor from the very depths of the rotting of the leaves, but the putrefaction does not reach them. That happens with her, or with some memory of her in the jungle, which becomes greater and greater, and she was great in a time he does not know but intuits. She, the prostitute, was sublime then, and he must know it somehow, it cannot be that he has spent and is spending so much time just to penetrate a woman's soul.]

AZ's own moment of transcendence, his destruction of the repository of oppression, restores *la otra* to sublimity as well. A vision of her, ascendant, overarches the sky, her spirit freed in the explosion. Both her political work and the demonic allure that involved AZ in the revolution have come to fruition.

In the novels of Valenzuela and Traba, and in Peri Rossi's poetry, there is an inescapable engagement with political practice. Exile can produce alienation and transcendence; it can be a metaphor for solitude, absence, femininity. But exile writing also needs to stay responsible to its own origins. That is the lifeline that allows textual acrobatics on the edge of space. Modernity can too easily become the sterile, self-referential text. Formal feats of derring-do, like Valenzuela's dancing Moebius mosaic of narrative voices and stances that approach and recede from authority and reliability, become resonant when experiential reality brought to bear from outside the text connects it to life. By seizing the language the exile writer rescues it from evisceration and acts to save the culture her language encodes.

4

Body/Politics: Alicia Partnoy's *The Little School*

> A survivor's testimony is more important than anything that could be
> written about survivors.
> Elie Wiesel

As resistance to the threat of annihilation, "presence" must be interactive. It requires not only speaker but also respondent, whose willingness to answer the cry of "Presente" affirms mutually held values and beliefs. In its overtly political engagement of both writer and reader, testimonial writing is an extended version of the revolutionary cry of, and call to, presence. In some instances testimony is written down and distributed by intermediaries. In Alicia Partnoy's case, the writer herself is the revolutionary presence who asserts herself and survives. Nonetheless, Partnoy's book is the product not only of her own experience and labor, but of that of other women as well. *The Little School* is an account of some of the experiences of the author and her companions in an Argentine concentration camp where they were held between January and April of 1977, before Partnoy was transferred to prison for another two and a half years.[1] The companionship among women so crucial to survival in *The Little School* is echoed in the collaboration among women who, as preface writer, editors, translators, and illustrators, contributed to the production of the book. Partnoy's book of tales is a product not only of the individual woman's experience as a political actor, but also of an international women's movement that elicits, publishes, and provides much of the readership for such works. Partnoy's publisher, Cleis Press, is a small feminist publishing company in the United States whose other titles include works on disabled women, incest, lesbian mothers, pregnancy and childbirth, and resistance to male violence. In its genesis, *The Little School* is similar to other Latin American women's testimonial texts, including *Nosotras también jugamos la vida: Testimonios de la mujer venezolana en la lucha clandestina 1948-1958,* a book of interviews with thirty-two women who participated in the anti-Pérez Jiménez underground, to which is appended a four-page list of names of other women involved. This project was undertaken in the late 1970s by two Venezuelan women, one a journalist and one a social scientist, who noticed that the history of their country's struggle against dictatorship in the 1950s had been written as if the resistance were an entirely male project.[2] Similarly, it was not until the 1980s that the noticeable absence of women's testimony to their participation in the ongoing Chilean resistance began to be corrected by feminist groups who have organized to collect Chilean women's accounts of their lives.[3] It is not an exaggeration to claim that two other testimonial texts, Domitila Barrios de Chungara's story of life in the Bolivian tin mines, and Rigoberta Menchú's life history, were both produced and are known internationally in large part because of the interest of feminist activists and women social scientists and literary critics working within the context of feminist theory and practice. Domitila Barrios's book, *"Si me permiten hablar"* (later translated as *Let Me Speak!*), for instance, was conceived at the 1975 United Nations's International Women's Year Tribunal in Mexico.[4] Both of these texts have been widely read and discussed in the international feminist community, particularly by academic feminists in the United States.[5]

Though women's participation in political struggle may not be feminist in impulse, these examples indicate that our knowledge of that participation depends heavily on the feminist commitment to value women's lives and work. A commonplace of feminist historiography is that traditional history is blind to the presence of women and deaf to their voices. Etymologically, "woman's testimony" is an oxymoron; the root of "testimony" is "testes," an anatomical requirement of all those whose witness might be accepted in a Roman court of law.[6] Feminist psychology tells us that the invisibility and inaudibility of women in public life make women themselves believe that their words, lives, and experiences are less valuable, and certainly less universal, than men's. Thus, it is not surprising that the testimony of women has only occasionally been offered and rarely sought or preserved, except in the context of a women's movement that refuses to acquiesce to silencing and erasure.

Yet there is a crucial difference between the above-mentioned works and Partnoy's: all these other works appeared first in Spanish, published in Latin America and only later in the United States, but Partnoy's book is a product of U.S. feminist publishing and has not, as of this writing, appeared anywhere in Spanish. For this reason it is a particularly useful book for discussing the position of the North American, English-speaking feminist vis-à-vis the Latin American writer.

To publish, read, discuss, teach, and write about Alicia Partnoy's *The Little School* is part of the feminist commitment to honor women's words and lives, a commitment that in the context of Latin American writer and North American publisher, reader, and critic, is not entirely simple. For one thing, in the Latin American left there is a profound distrust of feminism, which it often characterizes as just another manifestation of U.S. cultural imperialism. Whether or not Partnoy shares this view, the categories that feminist criticism would pay close attention to in her text are of secondary importance to Alicia Partnoy herself. She does not raise the question of gender as an issue, yet to my eye gender is inescapable in the experiences recounted in the tales. The solidarity among the women interned in the Little School, the threat of sexual molestation by the torturers, the protagonist's relationship to her daughter and to her husband, her consciousness of her body and its deterioration, the awareness that even in this state she might be vain, the experience of pregnancy and childbirth while in detention, all have to do with being a woman in Argentine culture and can be directly addressed by feminist analysis. Yet just as she shrugs off the relevance of her Judaism, Partnoy treats her womanhood as though it is of no particular significance within the context of the politics of disappearance.

What also makes a U.S. feminist reception of Latin American women's writing problematic is that North American feminists who are not Hispanists are often uncomfortable with and ignorant of the Latin American cultural context. Since Partnoy's book was published in the United States, in English, presumably for a predominantly North American feminist audience, this is a real concern. The centrality of politics to Partnoy's text is a locus of potential misunderstanding on the part of U.S. feminist readers. Despite having dismantled the walls between public and private, unmasked as false the rigid borders between self and other, and blurred the boundaries between autobiography and theory, Anglo-American feminists have not sufficiently questioned the category of opposition that holds the political antithetical to the aesthetic. The reasons for this have to do with prevailing cultural definitions both of the artist and of politics. Politics broadly defined suggests the primacy of relationships among individuals and groups, and political theory, especially on the left, may even subordinate the power of the individual to the power of the structure. Reigning U.S. ideology, on the other hand, holds society to be an aggregate of individuals whose behavior is explicable primarily in terms of their unique characteristics, and it casts the artist (here, the writer) as the prototype of the idiosyncratic individual. At the same time, Anglo-American culture popularly defines politics as a self-contained institution having mostly to do with running for electoral office that is of little consequence in people's lives. This limited definition of politics effectively displaces an understanding of the term that encompasses systemic power relationships that emerge in diverse and seemingly unrelated societal institutions. A culture operating on this definition will perceive action taken based on a systemically-defined politics as paranoid at worst and as the blind loyalty of the not-very-bright brainwashed at best, and a politically committed writer as a contradiction in terms.[7] This unexamined cultural attitude also helps explain why the early North American radical feminist rallying cry that the personal is the political (i.e., that there are real, institutionalized power relationships that structure our intimate lives) has, among white feminists in the United States, rarely led to its corollary: the political is the personal—that the official and unofficial structures of power and authority of the state get expressed in our day-to-day experience.[8] In the Argentina of the 1970s, however, national politics was played out on the field of the body in the form of physical and psychological torture, and life was indivisible from politics.

Partnoy's editors help fill the space between the Argentine testimonial writer and the North American reader with a fairly elaborate bunting of prologue, introduction, illustrations, appendixes, and biographical notes. Bernice Johnson Reagon's preface, which forges an immediate link between Partnoy's writing and the cultural work done by Sweet Honey in the Rock in their music, affirms the entwinement of art and politics. Reagon's preface also suggests a connection between black feminists, who do not subordinate race to gender in either their analysis or their practice, and women in liberation struggles in Latin America, for whom national and cultural identity is crucial.

Partnoy's own introduction further contextualizes the tales of *The Little School* for the U.S. reader with a short history of Argentine politics from 1955, the year of her birth. (That Partnoy was born in the year of

Perón's overthrow is coincidental but emblematic of the dense weave of politics and personal life in this text.) She also discusses her own political work and details her capture and removal to the concentration camp whose name gives the book its title. The introduction ends with a sort of epilogue to the tales, in which Partnoy recounts how years later she met the mother and daughter of one of the women about whom she wrote.

Three kinds of discourse are discernible in Partnoy's introduction: didactic, evidentiary, and narrative. The first two establish the truth-value of the last, which, since it is the discourse of the tales themselves, signals that the stories about to be told are true. The appendixes that brace the tales on the other side are a further reminder that despite the literary quality of the tales, they refer to lived experience. The stark language of the epilogues, which are there to communicate information about the prisoners and the guards in the Little School, has the double function of corroborating and extending the information in the tales. The epilogues function as a dispassionate, rational hook to the text that will prevent the tales from remaining isolated in that compartment labeled aesthetic.[9]

> *Conversation between the professional reader and the statistician:*
> PR: *You really ought to read* The Little School.
> S: *I already have.*
> PR: *And?*
> S: *It's good.*
> PR: *How, good? Did it feel different from reading fiction?*
> S: *Yeah.*
> PR: *In what way?*
> S: *(in that familiar tone of voice that says, "Sometimes you really ask stupid questions"): You know it really happened.*

I approached Alicia Partnoy's book with apprehension, not wanting to read the accounts of torture I knew it must contain. This was not going to be an ordinary literary text from which the accustomed critical distance would be possible, yet part of my fear was that as an accomplished reader, I might yet protect myself from the book's content. It seemed that I must either make myself vulnerable, however vicariously, to Partnoy's pain, or set up the barriers that would protect me from it. The first path seemed perilous, the second immoral. Then a third and worse fear surfaced—that I would find the descriptions of torture fascinating, even thrilling. Faced with the possibility of confronting my own complicity with the torturers, I let the book remain unopened for weeks.

My a priori responses to the book undid any neat distinctions I might previously have erected between ethics and theorizing discourse. If I could not yet find the courage to read the text, I could at least pay attention to the issues its mere existence raised. To what extent can testimonial writing be considered a form of literary discourse? What demands does it make on its readers? Can in fact a text demand anything, and if not, what is the relationship between author and text, and then between author and reader, a human relationship that might, in fact, make claims? And what could account for my multiple and contradictory assumptions about violence in the text?

Latin American testimonial writing has been noted for its nonliterariness, a kind of no-nonsense approach to getting the facts straight. Renato Prada Oropeza characterizes this stance as nonmanipulative, what some writers see as a kind of discursive manliness.[10] One way to prove one's masculinity after having undergone the disempowering experience of arrest and torture is to write on one's experience as a political actor and to do so without succumbing to an effete attention to language. Yet this approach is naive, insofar as it pretends to objectivity and neutrality in a highly emotional and ideologically determined setting. Ariel Dorfman, referring to Chilean testimony, notes, "this carelessness about language, the fact of thinking of it as a mere vehicle of a truth that is already preestablished, that is to say, as an instrument that is almost outside what is really important, such a way of understanding written or spoken language is one of the greatest weaknesses of the Chilean left."[11] Since few of the testimonies to come out of recent political struggles in Latin America have been written by literary people, to praise their artlessness may merely be a means of making a virtue out of a liability. It is not insignificant, however, that this liability achieves its standing as a virtue by dint of being codified "masculine."

Partnoy's book is not "straight testimony," by which I mean here reportage that pretends language is a transparent vehicle. *The Little School* deliberately blurs the boundary between story and history, so that the "tales" Partnoy recounts escape categorization. Anglo-American reviewers have variously referred to the pieces of writing that constitute the body of *The Little School* as "stories" and "essays," and Partnoy overtly abjures any clear genre demarcation with the introductory claim that "in little schools the boundaries between story and history are so subtle that even [she] can hardly find them" (18). One writer coined the term *cuentimonio* ("storimony") to pin down the elusive form of crafted personal recollection that cannot quite be called either fiction or nonfiction.[12] The artificial sound of this word betrays the uncomfortable marriage of two modes that lie on either side of that problematic divide. There is no clear demarcation defining testimonial discourse.[13]

This blurred boundary is particularly disquieting to the pragmatic North American reader, who takes facts seriously, but who for facts reads newspapers, guard up and emotions stowed. Creative writing (already coded "not real") is read as an emotional outlet. It is safe to open oneself to the needs of a fictional character, because there is no direct correlation between the imaginary world of the text and the material world the reader inhabits, no residual responsibility once the book is closed.[14] Partnoy's testimonial writing draws on her readers' emotions, insofar as it uses the language and techniques of prose fiction or poetry—but its referent is material reality and it therefore calls for a material response. When a text brings together the emotional charge that reading usually displaces onto fiction with reporting of real-world events, readers are confronted with a disquieting need to act on the facts on the basis of their emotional response to them. This process disturbs a deeply held North American attachment to dispassionate justice.

Given the current notion that all language is symbolic and therefore always fictionalizes, it is "theoretically correct" to undo the division between fiction and nonfiction (and by extension between testimony and literature). Nevertheless, the apparently naive insistence on distinguishing "what really happened" from "what is made up" is still very strong. In common-sense North America the single most meaningful genre boundary is that between fiction and non-fiction, and Anglo-Americans' unease with testimonial literary writing like Partnoy's is due in large part to the transgression of that boundary. Neither the pragmatic oppositional "either reality or fiction," characteristic of the United States, nor the semiotic elision of reality into fiction originating in Europe, is a satisfactory solution to the question of the truth-value of different discourses, especially when those arise in a Third World context. Both positions derive from binary oppositions that privilege one or the other term, making of testimonial writing either the enunciation of perfect truth or just another fictionalization with no more moral weight than a science-fiction novel.

North American pragmatism overtly opposes reality to fiction and values the former, while the Continental theory that all reality is constructed contains an implicit oppositional dichotomy (constructed reality/inherent reality). This implied opposition is analogous to the mind/body split that values mind over body, spirit over matter, abstract over concrete. Taking testimonial writing seriously, which means paying attention to its call for action in society, means a return to the concrete, to the body, and to the referent, as terms of value and power equal and not opposed to the abstract, the mind, and the signifier.

The interplay between Partnoy's tales, told in a fictional mode, and the ancillary texts—introduction, appendixes, author's biography—refuses to claim the superiority of either, but rather assures each other's complete comprehension. The ancillary texts are the concrete but skeletal frames to which the tales give depth and affective meaning. Nor is it that one form of discourse is less constructed than the other, but only that together they converge on not just the representation but also the communication of a certain reality whose significance lies as much in the affective realm as in the material. Perhaps the best example of how this functions in the book is the account of Alicia Partnoy's arrest, which is recounted in both the author's introduction and the first tale.

First, from the introduction:

> On January 12, 1977, at noon, I was detained by uniformed Army personnel at my home, Canadá Street 240, Apt. 2, Bahía Blanca; minutes later the same military personnel detained my husband at his place of work. I was taken to the headquarters of the 5th Army Corps and from there to a concentration camp, which the military ironically named the Little School (*La Escuelita*). We had no knowledge of the fate of Ruth, our daughter. From that moment on, for the next five months, my husband and I became two more names on the endless list of disappeared people. (13-14)

And from the tale:

> That day, at noon, she was wearing her husband's slippers; it was hot and she had not felt like turning the closet upside down to find her own. There were enough chores to be done in the house. When they knocked at the door, she walked down the ninety-foot corridor, *flip-flop, flip-flop*. For a second she thought that perhaps she should not open the door; they were knocking with unusual violence . . . but it was noon time. She had always waited for them to come at night. It felt nice to be wearing a loose house dress and his slippers after having slept so many nights with her shoes on, waiting for them.
>
> She realized who was at the door and ran towards the backyard. She lost the first slipper in the corridor, before reaching the place where Ruth, her little girl, was standing. She lost the second slipper while leaping over the brick wall. By then the shouts and kicks at the door

were brutal. Ruth burst into tears in the doorway. While squatting in the bushes, she heard the shot. She looked up and saw soldiers on every roof. She ran to the street through weeds as tall as she. Suddenly the sun stripped away her clothing; it caught her breath. When the soldiers grabbed her, forcing her into the truck, she glanced down at her feet in the dry street dust; afterward she looked up: the sky was so blue that it hurt. The neighbors heard her screams.

The floor of the truck was cool, but the tiles at Army Headquarters were still cooler. She walked that room a thousand times from one end to the other until they came to take her. Through a peep hole under her blindfold she could see her feet on the tiny black and white tiles, the stairs, the corridor. Then came the trip to the Little School. (25-26)

The introduction's version, almost entirely recounted in the passive voice, is at an emotional remove from the events that is challenged only by the single evaluative adjective, "endless," characterizing the lists of names of disappeared people. The version of this story recounted in the tale contains enough details from the evidentiary version (the time of day and year, the child's name, the arrest) to reinforce the idea of its factual validity, and the texture of the narrative—access to the character's thoughts and feelings, the contrast between domesticity and threat, the child's helplessness, the irony and vulnerability of being without shoes, the very embodiedness of the pleasure of loose clothes, contrasts of heat and cold—gives affective reality to the facts.

In the terrible years of the Yezhov terror I spent seventeen months waiting in line outside the prison in Leningrad. One day somebody in the crowd identified me. Standing behind me was a woman, with lips blue from the cold, who had, of course, never heard me called by name before. Now she started out of the torpor common to us all and asked me in a whisper (everyone whispered there):
"Can you describe this?"
And I said: "I can."
Then something like a smile passed fleetingly over what had once been her face.

Anna Akhmatova

The poet can describe the unspeakable, evoke the unimaginable. That, of course, is what I was afraid of in Partnoy's book. I understood the near-smile on the woman's face in Akhmatova's anecdote as the response of a woman who not only needed her experience validated, but also wanted to know that the nightmare could be put into words and there-fore somehow managed. For her, reading a description of the familiar horror would be part of a healing process. But for the outsider, the horror is first experienced in the reading and must cause a new pain.

In the experience of arrest and internment in a concentration camp, power is stripped from the victim and invested in the interrogators. The victim is dependent on them for all of life's necessities—food, clothing, shelter. The torturers exercise power over the victim's body in the functions of sleep, elimination, movement, sight, speech; they have literal power of life and death over their prisoners. In their access to forms of public discourse, they cast themselves as heroes and their victims as enemies of the nation. As torturers they almost invariably hood and hide themselves, but as members of the military and allies of the government these men had at least indirect access to an already controlled media that deliberately slandered and dehumanized their opposition. For the victim to put the experience of disappearance and torture into language is to exercise a form of control over that experience. This articulation at first seemed to me a private affair, of benefit to the participants in the drama. In addition, however, naming the experience for what it is presents an alternative interpretation to the official one to people not primarily affected, either as torturer or tortured. Certainly the use of testimony like Partnoy's in bringing charges against the military in Argentina cannot be underestimated. Still, the other functions of testimony, identified by Dorfman as "to accuse, to remember, and to encourage," ["acusar, recordar y animar" (194)] likewise seemed confined to the specific historical and cultural situation that produced it. But Partnoy's publication of the book in the United States, and in English rather than Spanish, suggests that the literature of testimony is not limited in this way. I was being invited into the text, however much I did not want to enter.

When I finally read *The Little School,* however, I was not subjected to a no-win choice of either being overcome by the violence of official torture, or hardened to it, or mesmerized by it. I finally realized that my initial fear was a result of the way in which violence is commonly represented in North American culture, that is, in order to entertain or titillate, or to shock, and always occupying center stage. Since reading a story involves a mental recreation of the action, in this case I expected to be thrust into a simulated experience of torture, with no bearable place to stand—not in the place of victim, of torturer, or of observer. Literary representations of violence elicit excitement in the reader, but in testimony they ought to evoke compassion for the victim and revulsion toward the act and its perpetrator. The victim cannot, as in familiar representations, be merely a passive object of suffering. She must be the subject of her story and apprehended as such. Alicia Partnoy, as writer and as protagonist, is a subject, and the reader led through her experience finds that the torture is there, and it is awful, but the torture is not all there is, nor is it foregrounded. The subtitle of the book is a true guide: these are tales of *survival,* and of how that is accomplished against a background of humiliation and pain.

I had been expecting to confront a representation of violence that was essentially pornographic, and what I encountered instead was a refutation of the pornographic imagination. Torture as an instrument of political repression challenges any pat psychoanalytic interpretation of sexual violence as an enactment of masochistic desire. Insofar as pornography complies with psychoanalysis's version of women's desire as masochistic, it relies on the inevitability of women's pain as pleasure and tells a story of pain that, by cultural standards, must also be pleasurable, the same way that the competent telling of any familiar story is a source of narrative pleasure. In *The Little School,* however, the pornographic story is not retold. Partnoy resists passivity and refuses to concede power to the torturers. Instead of being dominant in terms of class, access to knowledge, and in control of the terms of the narrative itself (as they are in Sade, for example), the torturers are reduced to the level of crude, unthinking, subhuman creatures who, despite their power, can be outmaneuvered by their victims. There is no doubt that intelligence, humanity, and courage reside in the victims and not in the captors, so that when a woman prisoner is forced to remove her clothes she can do so with dignity, knowing that the men who force her to do so are as worms.

Far from reinforcing the notion of the captive woman as a passive, no less willing, victim, Partnoy emphasizes the will to strength and the refusal to succumb among the imprisoned. The gaze in this text, unlike the pornographic gaze, is not focused down on the victim; it is the victim's and it is defiant. Her ability to maintain an ironic distance, even in the face of torture, further emphasizes her humanity and superiority. Partnoy's description of her captors' inept Chinese water torture, her sardonic refusal to be cowed by their threat to turn her into a bar of soap, with its implications of a final-solution machinery ["I'm convinced that at the Little School there isn't sufficient technology to make soap out of anybody" (61)], and even the irreverent nicknames the prisoners give guards all serve to disallow the authority of the torturers.

As the author of her text, Partnoy controls nuance, focus and point of view, if not the crude content of the tales. Consequently, the tales are highly personal and idiosyncratic. They range from the anecdotal to the reflective, but all are brilliantly lit and closely focused. Deprived of belongings, movement, and even of vision—the prisoners were punished if the blindfolds they wore constantly were found to be loose—Partnoy becomes a minimalist. The few objects she has—a pair of beach slippers, one of which is adorned by a ridiculous plastic flower, a matchbox in which she keeps a tooth knocked out by a guard, the gauze of her blindfold, the jean jacket that had been worn by a friend—become the objects of her scrutiny. What is lost in scope is made up for in depth. In the vignette entitled "The Denim Jacket," Partnoy evokes the sensual experience of wearing the jacket, feeling its warmth and protection, recognizing its limits (its padding only partly absorbs the beating she receives, and she cannot put her bound hands in its pockets), and she explores the meaning of courage, comfort, and friendship without losing sight of the death of the jacket's owner.

The tight focus on discrete objects that in other circumstances would be unremarkable (plastic flower, matchbox, tooth, jacket), the investment of emotional and aesthetic energy in unlikely places, is dictated by the constraints of the circumstances. This intense scrutiny directs the readers' attention away from the unlikely objects onto the empty spaces surrounding them, even as it focuses our gaze so powerfully on them. The virtual obsession with saving, eating, sharing, and playing with food draws attention to the paucity and wretched quality of the food, as well as to the deprivation of objects that could otherwise occupy the prisoners. Similarly, the episodic nature of the text in conjunction with its sketchy but faithful chronology forces our attention to the empty space— the events that occur between the tales. The illustrations reinforce this tension between presence and absence. Drawn by Raquel Partnoy, the author's mother, they both evoke and repress the fury of the violence.

Here we have variations on two familiar concerns of feminist criticism: the empty spaces in women's writing, and women's purported obsession with detail. Partnoy's empty spaces are emblematic of that which remains unspoken by women, a theme that has been explored by Anglo-American feminists as different from each other as Tillie Olsen and Susan Gubar.[15] Partnoy's attention to detail recalls the work done by Naomi Schor calling for "a clitoral school of feminist theory that might then be identified by its practice of a hermeneutics focused on detail."[16] The critical context shifts with Partnoy, however, from the sociosexual arrangements studied by Anglo-American feminist critics and the psychosexual constructs we associate with French feminist criticism, to the nexus of politics and gender. The torturer/victim dyad, a grotesque limit case of patriarchal hierarchy (leaving aside the actual sex of the victim, who is gendered feminine by virtue of being the prisoner), creates a monstrous caricature of the ordinary constraints on women.[17] The torturer quite literally limits the victim's field of vision and possibility of speech. What little is enunciated becomes luminescent for the concentration of gaze directed to it; the darkened, empty surrounding space, where the blindfold functions and the prohibition on speech holds, is starkly apparent to the reader.

Under these conditions, language is a highly valued commodity. Speech was a punishable offense in the Little School. Prisoners were beaten if they were found talking among themselves, and one of the great moments of pleasure and triumph is the conversation, protected by the muffling sound of rainfall, between Alicia and her friend María Elena. Language is precious and poetry is a pleasure to be treasured, though it can be dangerous as well. Alicia's husband undergoes a torture session in which the police demand to know the "real" meaning of one of her poems, and in one instance Alicia and the other "old-timers" indulge in poetry instead of relaying crucial information to some new prisoners, which results in the latters' being beaten for an infraction of a rule they did not know existed.

This last incident suggests that language needs to be construed as more than representation. In the theorization of language as representation, the reader needs to be active only in reassembling the image that the writer, or the culture, inscribes as text, in the way that a telephone receiver reconverts electrical impulses into sound. Although this is a necessary act, it undervalues the content of the image (or message) and ignores the consequences of acting or not acting in response to that content. With speech so constrained, communication goes beyond spoken or written language to include such means of expression as touch and the sharing of food. Language is not the only way of organizing experience into understanding, and knowledge depends on a material reality that needs to be interpreted, communicated, and finally acted upon.

5

Gaby Brimmer: A Life in Three Voices

The technical devices of fiction that Alicia Partnoy handles so deftly do not keep *The Little School* from being read as testimony. Conversely, the traditional collaborative process that usually marks testimonial literature does not quite make *Gaby Brimmer* a testimonial work.[1] Partnoy's public, political engagement with oppositional politics is denied to Brimmer, whose struggle on behalf of disabled people is neither quite the center of her text, nor yet even recognized as political.

Gaby Brimmer is a nonfiction text whose authorship is shared, but also contested.[2] It is a text that asserts the subjectivity of a disabled woman even as its multiple authors call the unity of that subject into question. *Gaby Brimmer* thus serves as an ideal ground for enlarging the ongoing discussion of subjectivity and representation within feminist theory.

Framed as dialogue rather than narrative, an amalgam of biography, autobiography and testimony, *Gaby Brimmer* is not easily classifiable. It might be described as life history, a form more closely associated with social-science scholarship than literary criticism. Since "life history" is a category invented by people not particularly interested in the form and structure of texts per se, to call this book "life history" is in effect to avoid the question of literary taxonomy while still saying something about the content of the work.[3]

Because systems of classification in literature begin with a notion of certain canonical forms and then work outward to account for even the most unruly texts, they can never be precise enough. All literary taxonomies tend to lose clarity at the edges and relegate certain borderline phenomena to anomaly. Since the classification of rebellious texts can in this way easily turn into repression, literary taxonomy should be looked upon warily by feminist or otherwise politically committed critics of Latin American literature. Insofar as literary identity (i.e., genre) is similar to human identity in that they both have to do with conforming to certain norms, and to the extent that borderline texts are analogous to marginalized people, the issue of classification is of considerable interest to feminist criticism. Moreover, there is a correlation between a genre and the prestige it enjoys and the status of the group to which its authors belong. For feminist critics these concerns have led to studies of the politics of canonization and analyses of the relationship between gender and genre, particularly in the reevaluation of the unprestigious forms such as letters, diaries, and popular fiction in which women have, historically, written, and which have, traditionally, been labeled "not literature." A combination of its subject matter and its form makes *Gaby Brimmer* part of this category of nonliterature, and though the book was a commercial success in Mexico it has been virtually ignored by a critical establishment that has given serious attention to other books signed by Elena Poniatowska.

The book in fact bears the names of two authors (Gaby Brimmer and Elena Poniatowska), despite which the text is presented as a conversation among three women (Gaby, her mother Sari, and her nurse Florencia Morales Sánchez). If the dialogue form obscures Poniatowska's role in shaping *Gaby Brimmer,* it at least indicates that her task was primarily editorial. Gaby's part in the production of the text is, ultimately, even more unclear than Elena's.[4] Though it is Gaby's life story, the book lacks the univocality of autobiography. On the other hand, the strong, often argumentative presence of Gaby's own voice keeps the book from being biography. Structurally, the text comes closest to testimony, but lacks the witness and denunciation of publically political events that are the primary force of testimonial texts.[5] Where *Gaby Brimmer* coincides with the Western tradition in autobiography—the affirmation of a unique self—it deviates from Spanish American autobiography, which, as Sylvia Molloy has shown, proclaims the representativeness of the subject rather than his or her individuality.[6] Gaby Brimmer, the person, is a Mexican Jewish woman poet with cerebral palsy. *Gaby Brimmer,* the book, is a partial, jigsaw-puzzle representation of her life. It is not incidental that they bear the same name. In a way, the book is a testament to Western logocentrism: The anxiety of Gaby's mother about the publication of the book suggests that Gaby's existence achieves meaning as she is constituted in and through language. For a woman whose ability to communicate orally is severely limited (only her nurse can understand her speech) and who stands as a glaring exception to orthodox womanhood, the ability to express herself textually means for Gaby the world's acknowledgment of her presence. By creating the textual body that is the book, the physical body can be transcended.

Western culture, which begins with a notion of normal from which any deviation is counted as a negative mark, can only see Gaby as an extreme example of alterity who is so thoroughly marginalized that she should simply not exist. She is severely handicapped and recognizes that most children like her are hidden away so as not to embarrass their families. She is first-generation Mexican, the daughter of eastern European immigrants in a land whose mythology says its people are a long-established mixture of Indian and Spanish. She is Jewish in a country whose story of itself as a Catholic people blandly occludes the presence of Jews within its borders. Her parents are Holocaust survivors: Austrian Jews who escaped a nation that was quickly overtaken by the Anschluss and more than ready to follow a leader who would obliterate the Brimmers and their kind, a man whose plan was that Gaby should never have been born. Gaby is a member of the urban middle class in a country that gets its richest sense of itself from its rural and indigenous landscape.[7]

Perhaps it is too obvious to note that while the world sees Gaby as other, she experiences herself as self. Yet this apparently tautological statement becomes less so when we consider the way hegemonic beliefs undermine the subordinated subject's sense of his or her own value and make the oppressed subject internalize a destructive sense of self. *Gaby Brimmer* is a counterhegemonic text insofar as it refuses the marginalization of the disabled woman. The Western model of the individual is a standard type—adult, male, European, heterosexual, financially well-off, able-bodied, Christian. As both norm and ideal, he is a creature who depends on an "other" against whom he defines himself favorably. In Virginia Woolf's memorable metaphor, he requires a mirror to reflect him at twice his size.[8] The struggle of women and of non-European, working-class, and other subordinate groups to affirm their agency and subjectivity meets with this culturally anointed subject as one of a number of obstacles. Their cultural definition as "other" means that they are already defined only in (a usually subordinate) relation to him, unable to be the "heroes of their own lives."[9] Yet for the subdominant class to claim characteristics of the dominant one is to suggest a denial of difference, perhaps even an alliance with the oppressor. In addition, at the very moment these marginalized groups are able to claim agency and subjectivity, the radical questioning of subjectivity occurring among European critical thinkers seems to foreclose on the concept.[10] Contemporary critical theory, nourished by psychoanalysis, calls into question the stability of the self along with the very notion of identity.

Mexican culture proposes a counterhegemonic mestizo subject with reference to Eurocentric thought, but that subject does not include women and is certainly able-bodied. In Octavio Paz's genealogy of the Mexican character, gender divides along racial lines that exclude Gaby.[11] The sons of the European father and indigenous mother are mestizo, but the daughters remain, like their mothers, Indian—passive and victimized. Ironically, Gaby's European (albeit Jewish) heritage, which could be an access to cultural centrality is precisely that which Mexican culture relegates to the margin. Gaby—white, middle class, intellectual, Jewish, angry, articulate, unable to do the physical labor of a wife or mother— hardly matches the image, either as ideal or degraded stereotype, of the Mexican woman. Yet Gaby affirms her national identity, refusing to be marginalized.[12] She will not consider living in the United States even though medical care there is likely to be better. Gaby describes the worst time of her life as the period when she was sent away from her family and institutionalized in Maryland. Not only was English the language spoken at the medical facility where she stayed; neither she nor the other patients were spoken to at all.

As a Mexican, Gaby identifies with Latin American revolutionaries, particularly Che Guevara, for whom she has named her typewriter/interlocutor. Her sense of usefulness and satisfaction in working for a cause greater than herself comes in large part from reading his writings. While Sari thinks in terms of her family's survival (understandable in an immigrant mother whose family has been threatened with extermination), Gaby assimilates into revolutionary culture that values collective action over individual achievement.

Being Mexican also allows Gaby access to Florencia's care in the particular way it is given. The Brimmer family is middle, not upper, class. Sari owns and operates a retail leather-goods shop in a fashionable shopping area. That provides the family with enough money to hire poor Indian women as household help in a society where rural poverty is endemic and vicious. The care Gaby gets from Florencia is not the professional medical care that enough money would provide in an advanced capitalist economy like the United States or that the health-care system would make available in a wealthy European social democracy. (Florencia deals with Gaby's most basic physical needs, but she panics when faced with a medical emergency.) The relatively high quality of Gaby's life depends in large measure on a system that maintains an underclass to take care of the private, physical needs of the rest. This class is largely composed of women, and the home-based tasks they perform are traditionally female. Although patriarchal, bourgeois culture denigrates the caretaker role (as woman's work), that work is far from intrinsically "low."[13]

The economic, racial, and social structure gives Gaby access to Florencia's care and love. There is no question that the system is exploitative, but that does not tell the whole story. Florencia's work engages her affectively. She and Gaby obviously love each other, and Florencia is far from alienated from her labor. Though the existence of an underclass is unjustifiable, it is also apparent that Florencia derives a real sense of satisfaction from the fact that Gaby could not have survived and flourished without the constant physical care she gives her. In this text Florencia's voice is clearminded and strong, as credited and respected as Gaby's and Sari's. None of these women was free to chart her life—Hitler forced Sari out of Vienna into a completely new sort of existence, and the racial-economic structure of the society created the parameters of Florencia's life, as cerebral palsy did for Gaby. The gender expectations of patriarchal politics further dictated the lives of the three. Nonetheless they cannot simply be categorized as impotent victims. Far from it: all three survived and even flourished under crushing circumstances. It is inadvisable, for example, to assume that Florencia was blindly and stupidly exploited. Florencia does not "live Gaby's life." She lives her own.[14]

Just as Gaby claims her national identity, she demands respect for her considerable intelligence. She does so despite being twice deintellectualized, once as a woman and again by virtue of her inability to take care of her own physical needs or to make herself understood through speech. Since muscle control is something most adults take for granted, and since it is something we watch babies develop as they grow, Western society tends to assume that the lack of bodily control associated with cerebral palsy is a function of a general infantile state. Most centrally, an adult's inability to speak is commonly misinterpreted as a sign of mental impairment. The fear of physical defectiveness, coupled with the notion of individual responsibility and the atomized self, induces in able-bodied people an atavistic belief (less a belief, really, than a wish that surfaces as intuition) that people with cerebral palsy are somehow at fault—as if they lacked the will to get up and act normally, or as if they were being punished for some cosmic transgression. Above all, disabled people serve as a reminder of the vulnerability of the rest of us. Florencia points out that both students and professors at the university were reluctant to have Gaby among them, demonstrating not only their impatience and extreme lack of sensitivity, but real ignorance as well. Many professors at the university simply denied Gaby entry into their classes. For her part, Gaby resists the double deintellectualization ascribed to her. Fully aware of the obstacles facing her, she insists on attending classes in the public schools alongside normal students.

> No crean que fue fácil, me costó mucho trabajo que me aceptaran. No me quisieron hacer los exámenes finales con todo y que era una alumna regular de primaria porque no había la seguridad de que fuera yo la que realmente contestaba. (75)

> [Don't think it was easy; it was hard work getting them to accept me. They didn't want to give me my final exams even though I was a regular student because they couldn't be sure that I was really the one who was answering.]

Finally, Gaby struggles against being doubly marginalized by virtue of her gender. Ironically, though she is subordinate as is any woman in a patriarchal culture, because her cerebral palsy fills the eye in a way that virtually precludes the viewer's seeing her body as sexually alluring, she is even deprived of her (male-defined) womanhood. If a woman is her body, then a severely disabled women is not, and yet still is, a woman. Gaby is, and is in, her body. Until she gets language, by means of an alphabet board her mother invents, and later an electric typewriter, it is assumed that Gaby is nothing but body, and a defective one at that.

A combination of the infantilization of the disabled body and a superstitious fear of contagion that is the basis of the repugnance for that body, makes Gaby sexually taboo. Since women's sexuality in Western patriarchy is defined with reference to male desire, and since that androcentric system claims that a desexualized woman is in a sense no woman at all, Gaby is effectively neutered. For Gaby, as for other women in such a sys-

tem, the body, beauty, sexuality, and identity are enmeshed. For her part,
Gaby claims her subjectivity as a woman complete with sexuality. Similarly, Gaby's menstruation is a source of pride to her mother, who sees it
as proof of Gaby's womanhood, evidence that she can bear a child.
Gaby's first words about herself describe her reflection — how she looks
to herself — and in it she sees an attractive body that is above all womanly:

> Tengo frente a mí a una persona, la veo en el vidrio de la ventana, sé
> quién es, aunque a veces no la reconozco. Es delgada y bajita de
> estatura, los ojos que lo dicen todo de su alma son de color ámbar o
> verde; según el vestido que tenga puesto. Su cuerpo está bastante bien
> formado y sólo le falta poder lucirlo. Mujer cien por ciento. (39)

> [I have in front of me a person, I see her in the glass of the window, I
> know who she is, though sometimes I don't recognize her. She is slim
> and small in stature; her eyes that tell everything there is about her soul
> are amber or green, depending on the dress she is wearing. Her body is
> rather nicely shaped and all she lacks is the ability to show it off. One
> hundred percent woman.]

Toward the end of the text Gaby returns to her bodiliness to claim outright an adult sexuality:

> Esto de ser mujer me está jodiendo mucho. No quiero decir malas
> palabras en contra de nada y mucho menos en contra de Dios, pero ¡qué
> juego tan rudo nos jugó la naturaleza y después la sociedad! Recuerdo
> mis palabras cuando reglé por primera vez: "Ya podré tener hijos como
> ustedes" y me dirigía a los pájaros que estaban cerca de mí en sus jaulas
> con los nidos que les habíamos puesto para que tuvieran sus crías. . . . Sé
> que soy mujer, he tenido orgasmos, mis deseos son tan fuertes que una
> sola caricia basta para provocar en mí un orgasmo, los tengo también
> cuando duermo, pero soy joven para conformarme con sólo eso; sólo el
> amor a medias, nunca la plenitud. Sé que entre más observe, platique,
> lea, estudie y me haga vieja, *voy a sentirme menos rebelde,* tendré hijos
> sólo en mis poemas y un día quizá sobrevenga la suerte de poder
> sacarlos a luz para que yo viva en ellos. Paciencia. Paciencia es la
> palabra que más odio, sinónimo de esperar, esperar, esperar. Sin
> embargo ¿qué otra me queda? (176-77; emphasis in the original)

> [This business of being a woman is really fucking me over. I don't want
> to use bad language about anything, much less God, but what a rotten
> deal nature handed us, and then society! I remember my words when I
> first got my period: "Now I can have babies like you," and I was talking
> to the birds who were near me in their cages with the nests we had put
> in there for them so they could lay their eggs. . . . I know I'm a woman,

I've had orgasms, my desires are so strong that a single caress is enough to give me an orgasm, I have them when I sleep as well, but I'm too young to be satisfied with only that; only piecemeal love, never plenitude. I know that by more observing, discussing, reading, studying, and growing older, *I'll feel less rebellious,* I'll have children only in my poems and one day perhaps I'll have the luck to bring them out so I can live in them. Patience. Patience is the word I hate most, synonym of waiting and hoping, waiting and hoping, waiting and hoping. Yet, what choice do I have?]

Gaby's sense that she must live her life through her writing is most clearly stated in this passage, in which she assumes that the only children she will have will be, or will be in, her poems. The passage also expresses the doubleness of Gaby's claim to a sexual self, since to experience her sexuality completely she needs the lover and resultant child simultaneously demanded of and denied her. Gaby's frustration and disappointment are somewhat mitigated by the fact that, as we soon learn, she is able to adopt a baby.

Along with her national/cultural identity, then, Gaby's intellect and her sexuality are crucial to her self-definition. The sexual and intellectual factors in her life are sometimes enmeshed, sometimes polarized, but they are always in some relation to each other. This is evident in the passage just quoted, where the source of Gaby's bitterness shifts from thwarted sexuality to the futility of writing.

Gaby's intellectual formation has its roots in the Western tradition that separates conceptually the functioning of the mind from the functioning of the body and values mind over body. Feminist philosophers and historians of science have shown how this dichotomy serves male dominance. Carolyn Merchant, for example, associates the mind/body split with a mechanistic view of the natural world under the mastery of man that emerged in the late sixteenth century, which relegates both woman and body to the realm of dominable nature.[15] Though the mind/body split, in which the mind is valued as that which makes man truly human, relies on the relegation of bodiliness to women, the fact that this is unstated makes it possible for women to appropriate the mind/body dichotomy when it is to their advantage to do so.

For Gaby, whose body overdetermines her life, the split between mind and body can be useful. Gaby can claim that her life is normal by focusing on the noncorporal part of herself and the intellectual/emotional experience she shares with able-bodied people who, nevertheless, can depend upon the body to enable the mind's life to function. Gaby, in contrast, must struggle with a body that must be cajoled into giving as much energy as it can to intellectual work. When Gaby must choose between mind and body—since the time and effort she spends on physical therapy cannot be spent on study, and vice versa—she elects to study.

Gaby asserts her subjectivity by associating herself with the mind/body split that privileges the mind. She claims normality in the most highly valued realm, thus minimizing the importance of those places where she does deviate from the norm. Nevertheless, as a strategy this is only partially successful, since there is no way for Gaby to escape her body, and her body requires her to acknowledge the relational character of her subjectivity. Gaby's definition of herself depends on what she can do, which in turn depends on the intervention of others. She simply cannot survive without the constant physical intervention of Florencia, or fulfill her social and intellectual desires without the social intervention of Sari. Her intellectual ability is real, but so are her pain and physical limitations. By intervening to mitigate the second, Florencia and Sari enable the first. Gaby represents an extreme example of all people's physical limits and requirements, and of the intellectual's adaptation to and of the environment in order to get on with the mind's work. Like the rest of us, only more obviously and drastically, Gaby lives in relationship and cannot survive otherwise. Furthermore, Gaby's decision that her cause will be "her people"—the handicapped—and her refusal to deny her sexuality, claim and affirm her body. By allying herself with the handicapped, Gaby also claims her body's stigma and makes it a feature of herself.

Feminist philosophers have argued that the concept of the disembodied mind is flawed and that part of its problem is that the mind that will not recognize itself as embodied is also blind to its connection to others. Susan Bordo characterizes the mind/body dichotomy as a manifestation of male anxiety about "a disastrously fragmented and discontinuous mental life" where "the lack of differentiation between subject and object, between self and world, . . . is construed . . . as the epistemological threat," and "the Cartesian reconstruction of the world is a defiant gesture of independence from the female cosmos."[16] Bordo suggests here that the same dynamic underlying the mind/body split fuels the urge to separate radically self from other. By showing how Descartes's bodily experience shaped his philosophy, she further demonstrates how, in fact, the mind cannot disengage from the body. Carolyn Whitbeck and others have argued that a notion of the self as not entirely independent can be derived from a female body-centered experiential base. These arguments offer an alternative to the modern Western notion of self. Another alternative model more readily available to Gaby comes to her through Florencia. Florencia gives Gaby access to an indigenous culture that sees difference differently. Each member of the community is seen as unique, and all are in some sense dependent on the others and on the group as a whole. When she visits the poor and working-class neighborhood where Florencia's family lives, Gaby is simply accepted as another person with her own particular set of characteristics and peculiarities that create certain needs. This nonhierarchization of difference is what makes Gaby decide that eventually she will go there to live. Whether she can live there successfully is another story. Gaby refuses to be passive or a victim and has none of the fatalism that to a certain extent underlies the acceptance of difference in Florencia's community. Outspoken and articulate, angry and demanding, Gaby pushes at boundaries and insists on her own ability, successes, and creativity.

Gaby claims a self that is both dependent on and independent of others. Her independence is reflected in her rebelliousness and impatience, her insistence that she is agent of her own life. But self and other have been redefined in this context so they are no longer mutually exclusive opposites. Gaby's very physical dependency means that she has to struggle to prove that she is not one with Florencia. When her professors suspect that Florencia is doing Gaby's intellectual as well as physical work for her, she must convince them that though her mind requires Florencia's mediation to make itself known, her intellect is separable from that of her nurse.

Here we have the makings of an alternative definition of subjectivity whose blurred boundaries preclude automatically characterizing an individual as "subject" or "nonsubject" (normal or deviant). Gaby's independence of mind, which must rely on outside physical support, has as its goal not a freestanding being, as Sari would have it, but a further connection with people outside her immediate sphere. For Gaby, selfhood is valuable to the extent that it can be incorporated into a social milieu that it can work to improve. Gaby sees herself as a politically active person whose politics derives from a sense of personal disillusionment:

> Para decir la verdad, yo soy anarquista. No me gustan los gobiernos de ningún pueblo del mundo porque poco a poco he ido desengañándome de todos y acepto que este desengaño fue muy duro. (109)

[To tell the truth, I'm an anarchist. I don't like the governments of any country in the world because little by little I have become disillusioned with all of them and I accept that this disenchantment was very hard.]

Her response to this disenchantment is not withdrawal, but commitment to a cause—that of the disabled:

Vivir para uno mismo no tiene chiste, ningún chiste. Por eso decidí que la causa de todos nosotros los inválidos iba a ser mía. (111)

[Living only for yourself is no fun; it's no fun at all. That's why I decided that the cause of all us handicapped people was going to be mine.]

The relationship between Gaby and her "two mothers," Sari and Florencia, indicates that the subjectivity and agency that Gaby claims must be relational. Gaby exists in and of a web of subjectivities, within which her own may be credited with privileged knowledge. The text embodies this relational selfhood in its conversational structure. The three voices often disagree; control of the story is contested. Gaby does not by any means relinquish her story to the others who take part in telling it. The relational self does not mean a self completely devoid of solidity indistinguishable from the others with which it is in relation, but rather involves an unstable system of boundaries that are sometimes blurred, sometimes sharp. Subjectivity is not, then, the same as atomization. (For that matter, atoms are in constant relationship with each other as they form and reform in chemical processes.) Gaby's attitude toward her intermediaries combines resigned appreciation and angry resistance. The very fact of her physical dependency produces in her an insistence that in all the important ways she is independent. Subjectivity is not stable but fluid. Sari's life is no more independent of Gaby's than Gaby's is of Sari's, and the same can be said of Florencia. They all know themselves and their meanings in relation to each other.[17]

Gaby's total physical dependence illustrates the fluidity of the body's limits, where these are understood to mean both what one is able to do physically and the place where one's body ends and the rest of the world begins.[18] Gaby negotiates the world by means of intermediaries. Florencia functions as her physical apparatus. She cleans and dresses Gaby, takes care of locomotion by carrying her when necessary, pushing her in her wheelchair, and acting as her chauffeur. She also reads, writes, and takes notes for Gaby when she enters the university. Florencia, physically close to the disabled woman, is the only person who understands Gaby's speech. Though she is saddened because the world does not pay attention to Gaby's needs, Florencia does not go beyond the bodily tasks I have outlined, and in fact often shields Gaby from social contact. Gaby interprets this shielding as obstructionist jealousy; Florencia says she is protecting Gaby. It is Sari who performs the function of Gaby's intercessor in society. When Gaby was a child Sari made sure that other children were around for her to play with and that they included her in their games. She looks for cures and treatment for her daughter's condition and knocks on government doors to obtain schooling for Gaby. Sari works to find practical, institutional means to make Gaby better and to insist that the world open to her.

Gaby's father, Miguel, opened the natural world to Gaby by taking her to the countryside to see and smell its beauty, or to the ocean so she could feel the water on her. When Miguel died there was no one to give Gaby the natural world for its own sake. Miguel also gave Gaby intellectual access to the world. His interest in philosophy and politics, which he discussed with his daughter, was instrumental in her intellectual and political development.

Elena Poniatowska is called in as an outside expert to facilitate Gaby's access to the society at large. The book that Gaby and Sari envision is another tool to make the world take notice. Like Florencia, who does the physical work of studying so that Gaby can be a student, and Sari, who negotiates the bureaucracy for her daughter, Poniatowska will do the work of composing Gaby's text and will use her contacts in the publishing world so that Gaby can be a writer. Poniatowska, however, does not see it this way. As far as she is concerned, she is the professional writer who can make a book out of a handful of poems and a series of interviews.[19]

Despite the deep affection among Sari, Florencia and Gaby, their relationship is openly conflicted. Within the text there are no apparent marks of stress indicating a similar conflict with Poniatowska, the agent who makes the work possible. Outside the text, however, these marks are evident. A movie was recently made about Gaby's life, without any consultation with or recognition of Poniatowska. This distressed Poniatowska, but Gaby probably assumed her life was her own to make a movie of, that the life takes precedence over the book. For Sari, the book was always Gaby's.

Elena Poniatowska was writing an article about Gaby when Sari and Gaby prevailed upon her to participate in the writing of a book that would include Gaby's poems. According to Poniatowska, she conducted a series of interviews with the three women, presumably taping Sari and Florencia and receiving typed or spelled-out responses from Gaby.[20] At one point in the text Gaby refers to the "letters" she writes to Elena. The text also includes several unmailed letters that Gaby had previously written to her friend Luis.

The text is presented as a dialogue, as if it were a simple transcript. But such clues as the interpolation of Gaby's poems and letters signal that the dialogue is constructed out of several kinds of text by means of deft editing and arranging, and not simply transcribed. Still, apart from the prologue there is no authorial narrative intervention, which feeds the fiction that the words of Gaby, Sari, and Florencia are unmediated.

This apparent self-effacement is a fiction. Nevertheless, though Poniatowska was aware of her labor and craft in making this book (as evidenced by her initial reluctance to dedicate so much time and energy to the project and her disappointment in being uncredited in the film), Sari and Gaby preferred to go along with the fiction and claim the book as Gaby's. Insofar as the book represents Gaby's life, this is understandable. And insofar as the book is meant to launch Gaby's career in journalism, it is similarly understandable, though the ethics of such a procedure are cloudy. Unlike illiterate memoirists, Gaby could write. She owned a typewriter and plenty of paper and had even seen some of her poems published. But she needed Elena Poniatowska's name to become widely known.[21] The question that remains unanswerable is if the skill required in producing the text was primarily Gaby's as a writer or Poniatowska's as an interviewer and editor. This is a form-and-content question that is complicated by the fact that Gaby did not simply provide Elena with oral testimony but gave her written text with which to work as well, and that in Poniatowska the line between writer of fiction and journalist is blurred.[22]

The unusual relationship between the subject and the collector of Gaby's story can shed new light on the ethical issues raised by the collecting and writing of life history. In most cases, the collector seeks out the subject, often for either scholarly reasons (as in the case of ethnobiography) or political interest (as in the case of testimonial). Most often the subject is a member of a national, racial, or political minority and (in consequence) less educated and of a lower socioeconomic class than the collector, raising such issues as, Who speaks in the name of whom? To what extent is the collector exploiting the subject for her or his own professional, economic, or political ends? What is the responsibility of the collector to the subject? Who is the appropriate signatory of the text?[23]

In *Gaby Brimmer* there is no substantial class or educational distinction between collector and subject, and the subject sought out the collector, not vice versa. Unlike the woman who emerges fictionalized as Jesusa Palancares in Poniatowska's *Hasta no verte Jesús mío,* Gaby resembles the illiterate, but far from unprivileged, authors of medieval memoirs who engaged scribes to take down their words. Poniatowska may have considered herself the "owner" of the text as professional writer in charge of eliciting and ordering the raw material provided by her three speakers, but Sari and Gaby thought of her as a hired hand—the best in the business, perhaps, but still subordinate to the text itself, and to the life it would validate. The question of ownership remains unresolved (Brimmer and Poniatowska share the book's copyright), but the way it is played out in this case indicates that it is not the textual structure of life history that puts the collector in a precarious ethical position vis-à-vis the subject, but rather the preexisting class difference between them and the weight of interest (i.e., who wants this text to be produced) that create this tension and possible imbalance. The question of ownership, which derives from an implicit Marxist analysis and informs the study of Latin American testimonial writing, may ultimately be less crucial to our understanding of these texts than what results from the relationship between recorder and subject and between process and product.[24]

Contemporary literary theory, which questions the relationship between the word and its referent, tends to sever the author from the text. *Gaby Brimmer*/Gaby Brimmer questions this radical disconnection. For Gaby and Sari the book is public proof that Gaby's life is meaningful. Gaby thinks of her published poems as vehicles for herself, through which she can live her life. Her sense of self is tied to what she can communicate about herself to the world. The text is not an entity in and of itself, but rather a medium through which she makes herself known, at the same time that it is part of what is known about her. In other words, Gaby will not disengage from her book. The text is part of her and she is part of it. This is a notion of text and author that flies in the face of contemporary orthodoxy in literary theory. Yet in a way, the author/text split is very like the mind/body split now being contested by feminist theorists. Just as corporal needs like alimentation, elimination, and reproduction, and their attendant functions and practices, seem to reduce the nobility of intellectual and aesthetic practices, the biographical messiness of the author gets in the way of the purity of what has been called the "disembod-ied" text. At best, the text is understood as existing in relation to other texts with which it is in conversation. In *Gaby Brimmer,* however, where referentiality is insisted upon by such means as photographs, corroborat-ing evidence, and journalistic technique, the book is vital testimony to the life of the subject/coauthor who, since she cannot communicate by speak-ing, makes herself known through the written word.

This is not simply a matter of self-representation. In fact, the multi-vocality of the text undercuts the authority of any single voice even as it enriches the reader's sense of Gaby's life with its contradiction and par-adox. *Gaby Brimmer* is also an attempt to communicate, to make con-nection between author/subject and reader by means of the text and to effect change as a result of the communicating act.[25]

Since what is at stake in this book is the justification of Gaby's life, there is a desire here to establish the truth-value of the text. But the pho-tographs, the famous journalist, the corroborating testimony, and later the movie turn out to be unreliable as proof. The photographs and the movie contradict each other. The family snapshots and the journalist's photos of Gaby are suspect as mere representations that change meaning as context shifts, and their value as portrayals of reality is further com-promised when the moving picture of Gaby shows us a different image of her altogether: the Gaby of the movie is an actress. The famous journalist is perhaps best known for her novelization of real people's lives, which calls into question the truth-value of what she writes.[26] The corroborat-ing testimony tends to agree on the facts but differ wildly on interpreta-tion. Gaby's book is not simply a transparent representation of her life, nor is it a fictionalization the way a novel would be.

On the other hand, the telling of a life that is at the same time the val-idation of that life can ill afford the deracination that comes from sever-ing the author from the text. Although it is valid, and I would argue ex-tremely useful, to call into question the relation of the authorial voice to the author to the speaker to the text, to lose sight of the fact that there *is* a relation is to deny human agency to individuals and groups who cannot bear further suppression and to absolve of responsibility authors writing within orthodoxy.

Here we can pick up the thread that connects *Gaby Brimmer* to testi-monial writing, which I first noted as a formal connection. This text shares with more broadly political testimonial texts commitment and in-tentionality. Gaby understands her rebelliousness as a manifestation of the same sort of dissatisfaction that drives social and political movements, and, as has already been noted, she makes common cause with other disabled people and is excited about the possibility of a movement to demand their rights as a group. (Perhaps not so) oddly, Gaby's story ends in a more conventionally happy manner, with Gaby's fulfillment as a mother. While there is no doubt that the adoption of Alma Florencia is of major importance to Gaby and requires her to make important changes in her life that most of us who are mothers will recognize (such as less time and energy to devote to other sorts of work), it is interesting that the happy ending Poniatowska gives this tale recuperates Gaby for the traditional femininity that she emphasizes at the book's opening.

Yet Gaby constitutes herself through her book by claiming her mind as well as a conventional femininity. Poniatowska's happy ending is gratifying, but too facile. The text has already opened up too much to allow it to stand unquestioned. Gaby, the writer, the poet, the student, must give up her precious reading and studying if Florencia is to have time to care for Alma. Where before Gaby sacrificed strengthening her body to expanding her mind, now she must again make priorities, and she chooses motherhood. It should be understood that no one of these choices can be deemed superior to any of the others, but it must be pointed out that in order to choose one, Gaby must foreclose on the others. Furthermore, the exploitation of an aging Florencia is simply not questioned in the text; her willing participation in the care of a small child is simply assumed. My point here is that Gaby is very much a child of her culture, choosing first the mind over the body and then motherhood over the life of the mind, and assuming without a second thought that her best interests are also Florencia's. Both of her choices, and her ability to achieve her goals—attending the university, adopting and raising Alma—fit easily into the culture's definitions of success and the preexisting class and race configurations that enable her to have that success. If intellectual success is deemed relevant to the disembodied mind, and if motherhood is the success of the feminine woman, then Gaby in a sense has had it all.

In contrast to Poniatowska, who organizes Gaby's story so that the claim of traditional femininity at the beginning foreshadows and predetermines its fulfillment at the end, I would like to offer an alternative reading in which, because Gaby as author refuses to sever herself from her text, she also frees herself from the need to define her success in the either/or terms of patriarchal culture. Mind and body both get their due; self and other do not remain apart. Gaby, always a self in relation to others, is no longer simply dependent; as a mother she is now depended upon, as the hero of her own book she can lay claim to her own story. Yet the relational self is troubled. It is marked by certain kinds of material exploitation, conflict, and simple—if cosmic—unfairness. A racially unjust society allows the Mexican middle class to make use of indigenous labor; a coproduced text's indeterminate ownership is the source of conflict between the collaborators, one of whom sees the book as her life's justification and the other of whom relies on attribution of her work in recognition of her professional status; the price of recognizing the self as relational is the pain and limitation of cerebral palsy. Gaby Brimmer's happy ending, her connection to others and what she takes from and has to offer to them, does not mask the ongoing struggle of her life or the lives of those to whom she is connected in personal, professional, or structural ways.

6

The Uses and Limits of Foreign Feminist Theory
Elena Garro's *Los recuerdos del porvenir*

The Little School occupies the ground between fiction and nonfiction, with its autobiographical tales out of school refracted through the poet's vision and the story-writer's craft, and *Gaby Brimmer* resists generic classification, but Elena Garro's *Los recuerdos del porvenir* is unmistakably a novel.[1] Its characters move through the recognizable landscape of southern Mexico, but their story is invented only in part out of the materials of Mexico's recent history. It is above all fashioned from the store of plots and possibilities of Western literary tradition. Although Garro invents two women characters who try to break free of the traditional stories, they are inexorably bound by them. One of these characters, Julia Alvarado, attempts to escape the plot written for her, only to vanish altogether. The other, Isabel Moncada, struggles to make herself present in history, but is relegated in the end to story.

Los recuerdos del porvenir is also a historical novel that takes on the very meaning of history, challenging Western notions of the structure of time. Garro does not so much either imitate or disrupt linear chronology as evoke a time that is whole and solid, as if it were frozen, but without the numbing effects of the cold. This notion of time derives from a number of sources: Western modernism's passion for formal experimentation, the Latin American novel's need to invent itself out of its own sources, the indigenous concept of time as circular rather than linear, and the difference in temporal mode ascribed to men and women in the West, where women have been associated with the unchanging natural world while men's production and creation have made History.

Julia Kristeva's essay "Women's Time" takes up this notion of gendered temporal difference.[2] Feminist criticism's desire to find its most compelling explanations in gender difference, together with the intellectual seductiveness of Kristeva's work, makes reading *Los recuerdos del porvenir* in light of Kristeva's essay virtually irresistible. Moreover, Kristeva introduces her taxonomy of temporal modalities arranged along gender lines with a brief discussion of European nationalism. She thereby makes "Women's Time" all the more appropriate in a discussion of a novel dealing with a crucial moment in the formation of national identity. Nevertheless, the Eurocentricity of "Women's Time," and of Kristeva's thought in general, puts clear bounds on her usefulness in discussing *Los recuerdos del porvenir,* and, I think, other Latin American texts. The limit lies precisely where Kristeva's abstract notions (here of history) become the concrete material circumstances of Garro's novel.

The implications for gender studies in Kristeva's theorization of the symbolic and the semiotic, her return to social and political questions, and the centrality of language (particularly poetic language) to her concerns, have made her work especially appealing to feminist critics, despite the fact that Kristeva only sometimes writes about literature and has declared herself not a feminist.[3] Indeed, in "Women's Time," Kristeva disputes the very existence of the category "woman" by questioning the notion of gender identity altogether. Now that the stability of the subject has been called into question and the sign "woman" has been "shown" to signify lack, Kristeva maintains, we cannot simply posit anything like gender identity, particularly for women.[4] As a psychoanalyst, however, Kristeva does operate within some notion of identity, however mutable, and no matter how unstable identity may be, it has the fixed limits of the body to work within. Since the morphology of the body is a crucial determinant of forming gender identity, gender identity ought to be one of the more stable characteristics of the individual. Under these circumstances we can talk, at least provisionally, about "women" and "men," the (unfixed but long-lived) power differences between these two groups, and the way those differences might be of consequence in thinking about writing. Kristeva's very title, "Women's Time," suggests that gender is still a valid category of analysis, and the essay itself is largely a discussion of European feminism, a politics that depends on a well-developed sense of gender identity, to say nothing of the existence of women. Obviously, Kristeva writes her essay as if women exist.

Los recuerdos del porvenir, first published in 1963, engages the question of the interrelation of time and gender that Kristeva later (and rather more benignly) comes to theorize. The novel is a melancholy meditation on the nature of time in a Mexican town battered by a violence that is made possible by historical events, but which immobilizes the town, negating its part in historical process. The interplay between the time of history and the time of changelessness and repetition inheres in the town's story of desire and futility so totally that the events of the novel can only be adequately addressed by taking account of the temporal modes within which they are understood.

The novel takes place ten years after the end of the Mexican Revolution, on the eve of the Cristero rebellions, in the southern town of Ixtepec.[5] Ixtepec is fascinated by Julia, the indifferent mistress of Francisco Rosas, a young revolutionary general charged with governing the town. When Julia abandons both her lover and Ixtepec, he becomes increasingly tyrannical, and the town increasingly rebellious and drawn to the counterrevolutionary Cristeros. In the course of a Cristero uprising led by Juan and Nicolás Moncada, the sons of one of Ixtepec's leading families, their sister Isabel becomes Rosas's lover. The brothers are caught, Isabel refuses the role of conventional heroine, and all ends badly.

Perhaps the most startling formulation in Garro's novel is a concept of extrasubjective time that is immobile, whole, and seamless, and which can best be figured in spatial language. Julia Kristeva has called this "monumental time," and she links it to the female subject and to the bodily apprehension of time as cyclical:

> As for time, female subjectivity would seem to provide a specific measure that essentially retains *repetition* and *eternity* from among the multiple modalities of time known through the history of civilizations. On the one hand, there are cycles, gestation, the eternal recurrence of a biological rhythm which conforms to that of nature and imposes a temporality whose stereotyping may shock, but whose regularity and unison with what is experienced as extrasubjective time, cosmic time, occasion vertiginous visions and an unnameable *jouissance*. On the other hand, and perhaps as a consequence, there is the massive presence of a monumental temporality, without cleavage or escape, which has so little to do with linear time (which passes) that the very word "temporality" hardly fits. ("Women's Time" 17; emphasis in the original)[6]

This self-enclosed, monumental temporality has resonances with the traditional novel, whose reader is attracted to a fictional world complete in itself. Garro accedes to this desire for the self-enclosed text, seducing the reader by bringing monumental time to the surface of her text. However, implicitly cognizant of the referentiality of the novel, which denies it the status of freestanding aesthetic object, Garro unsettles the reader who would escape into monumental time by showing how destructive it is to those trapped within it.[7]

On the formal level, Garro's novel is an exercise in monumental time. Its structure is what is commonly called "circular," that is, it ends where it begins. Garro uses the term *redondo* (round) to invoke that sense of completeness and impermeability when her characters experience immobility in time. Though the narrative follows a certain chronology insofar as the unfolding of the anecdote is concerned, the narrator frequently invokes other moments in time that are equally available, though less or more remote from the assumed present from which it speaks. These other times are evoked not to situate the moment of the anecdote within a greater historical chronology, but, on the contrary, to flatten out the differences between "before" and "after." The story Ixtepec tells is like a fossil imprinted in a stone. It is possible to read the stone's strata to learn when, in relation to other geological events marked in the rock, this particular one happened. It is possible to focus on that one fossil out of the many that there are. But finally, at the moment of narration, all of the fossils in the stone, no matter when they were imprinted, are equally present. Yet the story imprinted in the rock is not the result of natural history, with its intimations of inevitability and disinterestedness. The reading of *Los recuerdos del porvenir*, rather, is the reading of a rune, an exercise in the interpretation of an inscription that is already a hermeneutic act.

Garro invokes solid images of stone throughout the novel. Isabel, Nicolás, and Juan Moncada play statues as children; the night of Julia's escape the townspeople all freeze into position like children playing that game. The road Juan and Nicolás take home from the mines is a stony landscape that will later be the site of Juan's death. The madman Juan Cariño associates inaction in the face of injustice with the Stone Age, and Isabel prefigures her destiny when she impatiently calls her friends to return to their play rehearsal before she "turns to stone."

Kristeva's observation that monumental time is "perhaps a consequence" of cyclical time suggests how difficult it is for contemporary readers to enter fully into monumental time. Consequence itself is a function of linear time, in which one event follows another. We live in a period that experiences time as linear, and as much as we wish to give value to other temporalities, linear time pulls most insistently. We recognize, for example, the challenge faced by contemporary writers who seek to disassemble linear time in narrative. Syntactical language itself, as Kristeva points out, is a simulacrum of linear temporality. In *Recuerdos* we become increasingly aware of the way in which our knowledge of linear time impinges on our sense of monumental time, which in the novel is still bounded by history: the beginning and end of the history of the town of Ixtepec. Still, the very fact that monumental and cyclical time continue to compel us, either at the level of myth or at the level of our own bodies' knowledge, suggests that the linear temporality that is the legacy of the Enlightenment, positivism, and the industrial revolution has not entirely displaced them.

What may be less obvious is that the worldview underlying the experience of time as monumental has affected our experience of time as linear. Positivism's faith in objectivity (that given enough distance it is possible to get at truth) may well be understood as a holdover from the days of monumental time, when all time was spread out before God. Ixtepec partakes, symbolically, of the divine temporal vista, all its past laid out in front of it, as it contemplates itself from the shrine of the Virgin. But in the novel we come to understand that Ixtepec's knowledge, though vast, is incomplete. There is no ultimate perspective that allows for the truth. And if monumental time cannot afford that distance, how can historical time, always marching on, ever hope to?

Given the traces of cyclical and monumental time that appear in culture and demand our participation as subjects, it ought to be possible for the three temporal modalities to coexist. In *Los recuerdos del porvenir,* however, Elena Garro sets the cyclical/monumental modes into competition with linear (historical) time, with catastrophic results.

What makes the massive temporal perspective of Garro's novel at all plausible is the text's unconventional narrator, the collective memory of the town, embodied and disembodied at the same time.[8] The narrative voice locates itself in a real yet ambiguous space and claims for itself certain physical capacities: "Aquí estoy, sentado sobre esta piedra aparente" (9) ["Here I sit on what looks like a stone" (3)], as if it were a unitary, corporeal being. The singular "I" of this voice becomes plural, however, as it recalls its constituent parts. It frequently fragments into a "we," the many individuals who, over the years, have come together synergistically to constitute this collective consciousness. It sometimes distinguishes itself from those individuals, referring to them in the third person. The narrative voice knows what the people know, and knew, but it also knows more. From its vantage point above itself (looking down from the mountaintop shrine onto the town proper), the narrator has a panoramic view, both spatial and temporal, in which all moments are equally available to its memory.

In the monumental time of the novel, "memory" has an unconventional meaning, bestowed already in the title before the beginning of the narrative, a memory that has the future as well as the past available to it. Memory in *Recuerdos* is any cognitive movement in time, either forward or backward. If time is monumental, then not only the past but also the future is fixed and, given the right vantage point, knowable.[9]

Memory is what constitutes the narrator, according to its own account: "Yo sólo soy la memoria y la memoria que de mí se tenga" (9) ["I am only memory and the memory that one has of me" (3)]. The passive subjunctive ("se tenga") in that sentence, and the instability of a subject that must always revise itself in light of others' memories of it, expose the limits of that memory, however extensive it might be. For though the memory of the town is vast, it is not infinite. Ixtepec glimpses its own distant death:

> Y así las seguiré viendo a través de los siglos, hasta el día en que no sea ni siquiera un montón de polvo y los hombres que pasen por aquí no tengan ni memoria de que fui Ixtepec. (250)

> [And thus I shall go on seeing the generations, throughout the centuries, until the day when I am not even a mound of dust, and the men who pass this way will not even remember that I was Ixtepec. (243)]

The despair of this memory, which the narrator at one point defines as "an interminable wait" (152), contains the hope that one day its rocklike memory—the monumental time of Ixtepec—will crumble to dust.

> Hay días como hoy en los que recordarme me da pena. Quisiera no tener memoria o convertirme en el piadoso polvo para escapar a la condena de mirarme. (9)

> [There are days like today when remembering makes me sad. I wish I had no memory, or that I could change myself into pious dust to escape the penalty of seeing myself. (3)][10]

The collective knowledge of Ixtepec is more complete than the singular knowledge of any of its inhabitants, but it is no more reliable than the sum of its parts. Incidents left unexplained or partly disclosed to the characters implicated in them occasionally come to be understood after a lengthy piecing-together process, and sometimes are knowable to the narrator alone.[11] Hopelessly unable to know fully, the inhabitants of Ixtepec create fictions to explain the bits of information they have. Sometimes these information fragments, pooled and pieced together, explain events to the characters, but more often the collective memory knows what individuals never will. Frequently even collective knowledge is not sufficient, and only conjecture is available even to the narrator who, after all, is multiple but not infinite. What happened to Julia after she magically escaped from Ixtepec, and the reasons for Isabel's apparent betrayal of her brothers, are never known, though the narrator records various characters' conflicting assumptions. Julia is alternately believed to be dead or cavorting with a new lover, and she is observed, only to vanish, in any number of distant towns and cities. Isabel is called, variously, a traitor to her family, a self-sacrificing heroine, and the willing victim of a mad passion. Julia, always a stranger in the town, exists only as a projection of its fantasy. Isabel, once having belonged there, is no longer part of the knowing or the knowable after she crosses over into the space of the intruders by offering herself to Rosas. Even the words inscribed on the metamorphosed Isabel are ascribed to her. They comprise Gregoria's fiction of Isabel, not Isabel's account of her own behavior and end.

Since Julia and Isabel both have their voice wrested from them, the reader can never know exactly what happens to them. The silent Julia exhibits signs of what the reader will recognize as clinical depression: loss of appetite, weight loss, fatigue, withdrawal. These symptoms, however, can be apprehended only indirectly. Julia's beauty and the power that the townspeople believe she has as the general's mistress do not allow Ixtepec to perceive her as a woman with her own desires, but rather as woman incarnate, the repository of the desires of others. Moreover, the narrator is incapable of speaking from Julia's point of view, since she is by definition the unknowable, mysterious outsider. The other soldiers' mistresses, who are more closely connected to historical process and to Julia's own experience, believe that Julia's escape was abortive and ended in her death. The townspeople, on the other hand, in thrall to the mythic version, imagine her alive and thriving. In the end, Julia dissolves first into other people's oral narratives, reports of sightings, and then into nothingness. Isabel's fate seems to be the contrary of Julia's. She is literally petrified, turned into rock, the closest thing to stability and immortality in the material world. Both women, though, are reified, one through her dissolution, the other via her petrification. Both, finally, disappear as female subjects.

The other women in the novel count on their invisibility to make a political difference. The prostitutes and the old, impoverished Dorotea successfully hide the persecuted priest because they can cloak him in their assumed absence from the public, political domain. Similarly, the respectable women of Ixtepec believe they will be able to distract the soldiers long enough for the Cristero rebels to achieve their goal, because of the assumption that as women they cannot be political actors. That is, they too rely on invisibility. Ironically, they are brought down by those who are even less visible than they: their Indian servants.

Ixtepec is a town condemned to monumental time. Though historical time occurs all around it, Ixtepec remains still, making Martín Moncada's nightly ritual of stopping the family clock seem redundant. The one historical incident that occurs during the course of the novel, the apprehension of the antigovernment Cristero rebels, is not recounted. (How could it be? It happens outside the town, unwitnessed by any townspeople other than those who in one way or another have already left and are therefore beyond the scope of the narrator's knowledge.) As the rebels' attempt to crash history fails, Garro stalls time in Ixtepec by offering a series of three chapters that occur simultaneously. During the time that Nicolás Moncada is caught and his brother Juan is killed, the reader is constrained to pass through the same temporal interval in three different places.[12] This suspension of time is subtle, an author's trick, just as Martín's clock-stopping routine is, in his daughter Isabel's word, illusory. For "real" time stopping Garro gives us Julia's spectacular escape from Ixtepec with Felipe Hurtado, during which time, and therefore all action, ceases within the town, while conventional time continues outside it, as before. The morning following the escape dawns outside Ixtepec, but the town remains a fixed dark spot on the landscape, all its occupants frozen as if in a movie still.

Ixtepec's entanglement in monumental time is neither fated nor inevitable, however, but rather, ironically, the result of historical, geopolitical phenomena. A southern town, whose chance to move into history died with the death of Emiliano Zapata, it is controlled by men of the north for whom its entry into history would serve no purpose. The few inhabitants of Ixtepec who do try to enter historical time in order to push it forward are severely punished. Ignacio, the land-reform activist, is hung, along with four other nameless — and by extension timeless — Indians; the elderly don Ramón who dreams of progress through order and work is humiliated by Rosas when he tries to tell the general of his ideas about the future. Juan and Nicolás Moncada are shot by the government forces, and Isabel is turned to stone. Their mother, Ana, yearns for the violence of war to explode the unbearable sameness of her life, and her daughter and sons all inherit her desire for escape into possibility. Their dream is to get out of Ixtepec and bring change, i.e., history, back to the town. Isabel particularly seems both determined and doomed, but all three understand even as children that only death can bring escape. Isabel's protofeminist rejection of marriage stems in large part from her need to free herself from the cyclical time of menstruation, birth, and lactation that her life would become; the escape from Ixtepec with her brothers that she longs for would be an escape into linear time, with its promise of choice and freedom.

Historical time does make its claim on Ixtepec, but always as an intrusion from the outside, and never with any real success. The historical period in which the novel is set is the late 1920s. Calles is president and the Cristero rebellion is beginning. The soldiers garrisoned in the town are bearers of history, and most of their mistresses have real or imagined before-and-after-the-Revolution lives that are evidence of linear time. Calendar time erupts in the town, shockingly, at the end of the novel, at the moment of the executions of the Cristero insurgents and, ironically, to mark Isabel's definitive imprisonment in monumental time.

Of all the novel's characters, Martín Moncada occupies the most extreme position with respect to time. He interrupts time nightly when he stops all the clocks in his house, consigning his household to a kind of death:

> Sin el tictac, la habitación y sus ocupantes entraron en un tiempo nuevo y melancólico donde los gestos y las voces se movían en el pasado. Doña Ana, su marido, los jóvenes y Félix se convirtieron en recuerdos de ellos mismos, sin futuro, perdidos en una luz amarilla e individual que los separaba de la realidad para volverlos sólo personajes de la memoria. (19)

> [Without the ticking, the room and its occupants entered a new and melancholy time where gestures and voices moved in the past. Doña

Ana, her husband, the children, and Félix were changed into memories
of themselves without a future, lost in a yellow, individual light that
separated them from reality to make them only personages of memory.
(14)]

Martín's refusal to function within linear time makes him an economic
failure. Capitalism, after all, depends on the notion of progress. As a result of his inability to participate in the economy or in history, Martín's
sons have to work in the mines. High social class and racial caste do not
preclude poverty. Ironically, if Martín is to survive at all, he has to rely on
his servant, Félix, to be his everyday memory. Living in nonlinear time,
ignoring historical reality, becomes a luxury that can be indulged in only
at the expense of an underclass—here the Indian servants—and at the
cost of the family's economic survival.

For his part, Félix recognizes his own oppression in temporal terms
that echo the hopeless solidity of eternal time. He witnesses the cruel and
angry racism of his master's friends, spoken by them as if he were not
present:

Félix, sentado en su escabel, los escuchaba impávido. "Para nosotros, los
indios, es el tiempo infinito y de callar," y guardó sus palabras. (26)

[Félix, sitting on his stool, listened to them without flinching. "For us,
the Indians, the time to be silent is infinite," and he refrained from
speaking. (22)]

Though the Indians are, as Félix indicates, virtually silent in this novel,
they are present everywhere. They are the victims of antiagrarian reform
hangings. They are in the market, they travel from town to town, they are
the servants. Garro's criticism of the mestizos' indifference to the Indians'
humanity is structural: she turns the plot on it. The institutionalized invisibility of the Indian servant gives Rosas access to the details of the conspiracy her employers are planning. At the same time, however, the Indians' supposedly non-Western way of being in time is appropriated by the
novel's author for her main characters, the ever-less-affluent middle-class
mestizo citizens of Ixtepec.[13]

Martín Moncada's life adventure with time began at the age of five,
when he first confronted death. Death is the logical end of linear time,
and, as Kristeva notes, linear time must necessarily stumble against the
inevitability of that ending, making it obsessional, a time that must be
controlled. But Martín abjures control, recognizes the multiplicity of
time, and understands any linear movement in time to be retrogressive,

toward death, not progressive. Martín Moncada stops his clocks not to control linear time, but rather to disconnect himself from it so he can experience "the other time that lived within him" (15). Reality, i.e., that which occurs in time, is vast and collective; thus Martín's most useful and vivid memories are those that he himself never experienced. Furthermore, it is in memory that Martín senses the possibility of liberation from a cyclical temporality, which, because they do not understand its connection to the eternal, the people of Ixtepec experience as meaningless.

> Le gustaban los días festivos. La gente deambulaba por la Plaza hechizada por el recuerdo olvidado de la fiesta; de ese olvido provenía la tristeza de esos días. "Algún día recordaremos," se decía con la seguridad de que el origen de la fiesta, como todos los gestos del hombre, existía intacto en el tiempo y bastaba un esfuerzo, un querer ver, para leer en el tiempo la historia del tiempo. (20-21)

> [He liked holidays. The people wandered about the plaza, bewitched by the forgotten memory of the fiesta; from that forgetting came the sadness of those days.
> "Someday we shall remember, we shall remember," he said to himself with the certainty that the origin of the fiesta, like all man's acts, existed intact in time and that only an effort, a desire to see, was necessary in order to read in time the history of time. (15-16)]

Martín's hope for ending the town's sadness, for coming to knowledge, has as its precondition a monumental time in which each authentic gesture is preserved, as if in amber. Then all that is necessary is an act of will, the necessary desire to find—remember—that which is always already there. Martín believes he can approach this state by stopping the clocks, by making the symbolic gesture that obliterates movement in time.

In his evasion of clock time, Martín also escapes the calendar, which likewise would trap him in "un tiempo anecdótico" ["anecdotal time" (20)]; he meanders in a kind of eternal/cyclical time, when "un lunes era todos los lunes" ["one Monday was all Mondays" (15)] and words escape syntax and become magic—things in themselves and not part of a sign system that separates being from meaning.[14]

The association of the different ways language means with the different ways that time is experienced once again recalls Julia Kristeva. In *Revolution in Poetic Language* Kristeva differentiates the *semiotic*, associated with the mother/infant dyad in which there is no separation between self and other and in which the infant experiences the world as one with itself, and the *symbolic,* characterized by the child's separate existence from the mother/world and initiation into language and the world of the father. Experience of the semiotic coincides with monumental time. Both are totalizing, complete in themselves. Linear time, the time of causation and logic, responds to the symbolic. The list of binary oppositions would seem to sort itself out all too readily: semiotic/symbolic, feminine/masculine, monumental time/linear time, indigenous culture/European culture, myth/history, primitive/civilized, indivisibility/differentiation.

But Kristeva refuses to link the semiotic with the feminine, maintaining, on the contrary, that the semiotic is precisely that which, because it is not differentiated, is not gendered.[15] Furthermore, as we have already seen, linear time does not fully obliterate cyclical and monumental time; binary oppositions are more apparent than real, two points on a continuous, if suppressed, line. The semiotic remains even after the child's entry into the symbolic. Moreover, just as history determines one's temporal mode, even as entry into history marks the passage from monumental to linear time; language, characteristic of the symbolic realm and the entry into which is the great divide between the symbolic and the semiotic, is also the bridge connecting them. As Kristeva shows, signification requires the *interplay* of the symbolic and the semiotic. The sophisticated writer experiments in language to get beyond language. The semiotic is accessible through language by means of such cultivated tropes as metaphor, puns, and other forms of soundplay, neologisms: a conscious effort to achieve the mother lode of preconscious knowledge.

The characters in *Recuerdos* do not line up readily on one or the other side of the binary divide. Francisco Rosas, who as revolutionary general in command of Ixtepec is charged with bearing history, is uninterested in revolution, in history, even in power:

> Era el tiempo de la Revolución, pero él no buscaba lo que buscaban sus compañeros villistas, sino la nostalgia de algo ardiente y perfecto en que perderse. (78)

> [It was the time of the Revolution, but he was not seeking the same thing his companions, followers of Villa, were after; instead he longed for something ardent and perfect. (73)]

The embodiment of the Revolution, the man in charge of administering vast social change, wants nothing more than to merge with cosmic oneness. He does this first by means of his obsessive love for Julia, who he believes lives in an all-encompassing realm just beyond his reach. Julia passively submits to Rosas's physical demands, but she remains elusive. Julia's very passivity keeps her lover at a distance, since she offers him only the smooth surface of her body, but nothing of her self that he might engage. Julia's silence infuriates Rosas, but in a perverse way it is an emblem of the prelinguistic, seamless realm he yearns for. Later, taking Nicolás as his prisoner and Isabel as his lover, Rosas tries to immerse himself in the semiotic by entering the apparently self-contained, self-sufficient world of the Moncadas. The Moncadas, though, are fleeing that world, and Rosas is their road out. When Nicolás forces Rosas to execute him, he forecloses on the general's ever entering the charmed circle of the semiotic.

On the other hand, the women in the novel are not easily relegated to cyclical/monumental time. The soldiers' mistresses plot escape and change, and the prostitutes participate in the Cristero conspiracy. Even the proper mestiza women resist the cyclical/monumental time, both in their conspiratorial activities and, on a more personal level, in their resistance to monumental/cyclic demands of reproduction. The most conventional of the mestizas, Elvira Montúfar, is secretly delighted that her daughter Conchita resists her efforts to marry her off.

Unlike European feminist theorists like Hélène Cixous, who exalts in the possibility of finding and mining the feminine psychic space preserved in the semiotic and experienced in cyclical/monumental time, or even Kristeva, who sees the return to the semiotic by means of nonsyntactic use of language a liberating move by women and men alike, Garro unmasks the semiotic as a prison and monumental time as a form of hell.[16] The events she chooses for narration are those that immobilize Ixtepec:

> En esos días era yo tan desdichado que mis horas se acumulaban informes y mi memoria se había convertido en sensaciones. La desdicha como el dolor físico iguala los minutos. Los días se convierten en el mismo día, los actos en el mismo acto y las personas en un solo personaje inútil. El mundo pierde su variedad, la luz se aniquila y los milagros quedan abolidos. La inercia de esos días repetidos me guardaba quieto, contemplando la fuga inútil de mis horas y esperando el milagro que se obstinaba en no producirse. El porvenir era la repetición del pasado. Inmóvil, me dejaba devorar por la sed que roía mis esquinas. Para romper los días petrificados sólo me quedaba el espejismo ineficaz de la violencia, y la crueldad se ejercía con furor sobre las mujeres, los perros callejeros y los indios. Como en las tragedias, vivíamos dentro de un tiempo quieto y los personajes sucumbían presos en ese instante

detenido. Era en vano que hicieran gestos cada vez más sangrientos. Habíamos abolido al tiempo. (62-63)

[In those days I was so miserable that my hours accumulated shapelessly and my memory was transformed into sensations. Unhappiness, like physical pain, equalizes the minutes. All days seem like the same day, acts become the same act, and all persons are a single useless person. The world loses its variety, light is annihilated, and miracles are abolished. The inertia of those repeated days kept me quiet as I contemplated the vain flight of my hours and waited for the miracle that persisted in not happening. The future was the repetition of the past. Motionless, I let myself be consumed by the thirst that rankled at my corners. To disperse the petrified days all I had was the ineffectual illusion of violence, and cruelty was practiced furiously on the women, stray dogs, and Indians. We lived in a quiet time and the people, like the actors in a tragedy, were caught in that arrested moment. It was in vain that they performed acts which were more and more bloody. We had abolished time. (58)]

In this extreme situation, time-as-movement is abolished; intellect dies along with a logical structure of time. Memory is no longer thought, reason, and reflection, but a jumble of sensations. History is figured as miracle, beyond the scope of human will or action, parodied in gestures of violence. Though the reader, as privileged knower, can reflect on this stagnation, the subject caught within it cannot. To say that the future is a repetition of the past is to say that only mythic (i.e., always already known) explanations are available to make sense of the events of the present, which in turn preordains the course of the future. The experience of monumental time from within is the experience of being outside time, of having no past, no future, no hope; of living the useless accumulation of hours that Ixtepec describes. Only Martín, who has learned to function within it and who in fact invokes it, experiences monumental time as something desirable. As a local patriarch, Martín has the luxury of enjoying his forays into monumental time: his servant takes care of his immediate physical needs, and his sons take care of his economic ones.

Only the already privileged can take advantage of monumental time, and they can do so only at the expense of others. The utopian possibilities that some European and North American feminists ascribe to "feminine" modes of being willfully ignore the material reality of those whose historically specific material reality constrains them to living within those modes. There is no better way to perpetuate systems of oppression than to make them seem inevitable. Garro's text demonstrates how dangerous it is to romanticize, and how irresponsible to metaphorize, notions like monumental time.

Linear time offers hope for change, for breakout, but Garro's characters seem incapable of entering it. Even the Moncada sons become Cristeros not because they believe in the cause—in fact they think the Church is in league with the landlords and, if returned to power, likely to be as repressive as the corrupt Revolution—but because this seems their only way to escape. Much like Rosas, who has used the Revolution to try to escape historical time, the Moncadas intend to use the counterrevolution (which in its emphasis on restoring Church authority privileges eternal time) to break into a temporality that promises change. Exploding the monument—the earthquake or train wreck that Ana Moncada yearns for—seems the only way to make this break, but the narrator both shows and tells us that the violence keeps increasing, and there is no change.

Part 2 of the novel contains the possibility of the miracle, the hope that something will happen. The Cristeros are beginning to organize in the mountains; the town is outraged when Rosas closes down the church, burns the statue of the Virgin, and installs governmental offices in the sanctuary. Félix even forgets to stop the clocks. Nevertheless, Ixtepec never quite acts. Even its traces of historical action are figured as lack instead of presence. We see the church square after, not during, the massacre of the religious protesters, and the mystery of the sacristan, who seems to have been murdered, revolves around his *missing* body. The soldiers' ambush of the Cristeros takes place off the page, at the same time that three chapters take place in enclosed spaces, associated with the women of Ixtepec: the respectable home of Carmen B. Arrieta, the Hotel Jardín (where the officers' mistresses live and dream their abortive escape), and the brothel. As if by definition, history happens outside of Ixtepec, and the women's frenetic activity only circles back on itself.

Since neither the soldiers under Rosas nor the leading families led by the Moncadas can or will take hold of historical time, the town is at the mercy of those who will use history and politics for their own purposes. Only the parasitic landowner, Rodolfito Goríbar, travels freely between the capital and Ixtepec, manipulating events to increase his landholdings. Rodolfito is locked into an infantile relationship with his mother, who protects him against the world he so viciously despoils. This mother/son dyad is a caricature of the mother/infant relationship in which, according to Kristeva, the semiotic realm is experienced. Thus, far from entering the symbolic realm and historical time, which requires separation from the mother, Rodolfito feeds off the stagnation of the semiotic/monumental, and his perversion of the Revolution acts as a drag on history. The socially critical reading of these characters is inseparable from psychoanalytic and mythic readings. Both Rodolfito and his mother Lola are grotesquely fat. Their narcissistic self-indulgence is figured as a form of oral gratification in which they swallow up the land and destroy its inhabitants. In their relationship, this mother/son dyad monopolizes both time and space, a modern incarnation of Kronos and Gea as evoked by Kristeva:

> All encompassing and infinite like imaginary space, [monumental]
> temporality reminds one of Kronos in Hesiod's mythology, the
> incestuous son whose massive presence covered all of Gea. ("Women's
> Time" 16)

Garro's novel is laden with mythic echoes. It is narrated from the vantage point of the shrine of the Virgin, the primordial goddess brought forward into Christianity. The monumentality of stone-Isabel, the eternal mother/maiden who is Mary, the unchangeable story told by the rock at the shrine, all converge here. Gregoria, who has labored to place the monument at the shrine, is a reminder of Sisyphus, pushing his stone up the mountain. Unlike the stone of the original myth, which rolls back down the mountain and condemns Sisyphus to labor eternally, the Isabel stone remains, an offering to the Virgin. The story inscribed in the stone, the story of woman's sexual treachery, is condemned to repetition, as the town must live and relive its time because it cannot escape that preexisting myth.

Gregoria, the *curandera*, works in magic and the body. She demands that Isabel play the part of the canonical heroine who will redeem her brother; she claims to have witnessed the metamorphosis of Isabel; and she authors the story—accepted by the narrator—that Isabel was turned to stone in punishment for weakness of the flesh (her passion for the enemy Rosas outweighing both her loyalty to her family and her promise to the Virgin). Gregoria ascribes this fiction to Isabel as she inscribes it in the rock that the young woman has become. Gregoria's text becomes Isabel's, told in the first person and occupying the privileged place of "last word" in the novel.

> Soy Isabel Moncada, nacida de Martín Moncada y de Ana Cuétara de
> Moncada, en el pueblo de Ixtepec el primero de diciembre de 1907. En
> piedra me convertí el cinco de octubre de 1927 delante de los ojos

espantados de Gregoria Juárez. Causé la desdicha de mis padres y la muerte de mis hermanos Juan y Nicolás. Cuando venía a pedirle perdón a la Virgen que me curara del amor que tengo por el general Francisco Rosas que mató a mis hermanos, me arrepentí y preferí el amor del hombre que me perdió y perdió a mi familia. Aquí estaré con mi amor a solas como recuerdo del porvenir por los siglos de los siglos. (295)

[I am Isabel Moncada, the daughter of Martín Moncada and Ana Cuétara de Moncada, born in the town of Ixtepec on December 1, 1907. I turned to stone on October 5, 1927, before the startled eyes of Gregoria Juárez. I caused the unhappiness of my parents and of my brothers Juan and Nicolás. When I came to ask the Virgin to cure me of my love for General Francisco Rosas, who killed my brothers, I repented and preferred the love of the man who ruined me and ruined my family. Here I shall be, alone with my love, as a memory of the future, forever and ever. (288-89)]

Thus are we left with the predictable story of the perfidious heroine that forever consigns Isabel to monumental time. She becomes, quite literally, a monument to the old story of the danger of female sexuality; her story, that of a wild young woman willing to sacrifice her family to her evil lover, was knowable—a familiar woman's story of sexual crime and punishment—before Gregoria gouged it into Isabel's flesh-made-stone. Isabel is, bodily, a "recuerdo del porvenir"—not just a "memory of the future," but a "reminder for the future," a cautionary tale ventriloquized by Gregoria. The town seems willing to accept and repeat this tale as Isabel's own, since it begins and ends its story with this "piedra aparente."[17] Ixtepec describes Isabel on the day of her transformation, as she is diminished in anticipation of her essential moment. She loses her past and her future, all her time is refined to the single point, the crucial instant that fixes the essentialized Isabel:

El futuro no existía y el pasado desaparecía poco a poco. Miró al cielo fijo y al campo imperturbable e idéntico a sí mismo: redondo, limitado por dos noches iguales. Isabel estaba en el centro del día como una roca en la mitad del campo. . . . Gregoria le hablaba desde un mundo ligero y móvil que ella ya no compartía. (292)

[The future did not exist and the past was gradually disappearing. She looked at the glazed sky and the countryside, imperturbable and identical to it: round, limited by mountains as permanent as that round day, which was limited by two identical nights. Isabel was in the center of the day like a rock in the middle of the countryside. . . . Gregoria was

speaking to her from an airy, glancing world she no longer shared.
(285)]

It is then a short step from the lyric simile, Isabel "like a rock in the
middle of the countryside," to her mythic metamorphosis into that
rock.[18] Here is the dark side of perfection, of becoming the irreducible
one. This is not fusion with the universe in some monumental time, but
becoming the monument, the immobile bearer of one's own myth.

The novel ends here, but the end pulls us back to the beginning, and to
the middle. Gregoria is an unreliable narrator; the story she ascribes to
Isabel is most probably wrong. Even the inscription she carves into the
Isabel stone is false. Gregoria had lost sight of the young woman as she
ran down the mountain, and only later did the old *curandera* find the
stone she named Isabel Moncada. Moreover, Gregoria earlier misunder-
stood Rosas's obsession with Julia, believing that it must have been in-
duced by magic. She misread Isabel's relationship with Rosas, which had
to do with neither love nor self-sacrifice but rather was a complex matter
of destruction and self-destruction. Isabel did not betray Nicolás by taking Rosas as her lover; she and her brother maintained their connection
through their hold on Rosas, and together they compelled him to destroy
them and himself.

The primal couple in this novel is not Isabel and Rosas, but rather Isabel and Nicolás, the irreducible sibling pair, complete in and of themselves. Their separation is impossible, and in them Rosas sees both the
possibility for, and the utter impossibility of, salvation.[19] Isabel's story is
never fully known, but certainly is more complicated than the one Gregoria writes, not out of Isabel's life, but out of the store of stories available to heroines.[20] By all rights, the only one to whom Gregoria's story
should make sense is the madman, Juan Cariño, whose madness consists
in part of believing that spoken words can become solid and do physical
harm. Yet all the town, and most of Garro's readers, have accepted Gregoria's explanation.[21]

Isabel's magic transformation at the end of the novel is the analogue of
Julia's magical escape from Ixtepec at the end of part 1. In Julia's case,
time is frozen; in Isabel's the woman herself is. Both events are equally
improbable in phenomenal reality, yet the sources of these stories suggest
that we ought to believe one more readily than the other. Ixtepec knows
Isabel's story only through the unreliable Gregoria, but the stopping of
time that permitted the lovers' escape is corroborated by an outsider. The

narrator itself cannot say for sure what happened that night. Only the mule-driver who comes upon the dark town with its statue-inhabitants in the midst of the dawning countryside witnesses Julia's escape. The reader, like the mule-driver, is the outsider who comes upon the frozen town/text and must make sense of it.

Still, Julia and Isabel are ultimately denied their presence. Julia is known to the town only as a compelling sexual force, but she herself is alienated from her body until the man who knows that she has history, i.e., meaning beyond the sexual meaning invested in her by Rosas and the townspeople, causes her to vanish from them, as if by magic.[22] Isabel is similarly removed once the town no longer can conceptualize her. The radical absence of these two women is a function of history and outside forces, not a problem deriving from their own psychology. Julia never speaks, and Isabel is voluble, but in the end neither is permitted to represent herself.

7

Sylvia Molloy's Lesbian Cartographies
Body, Text, and Geography

The repression of women's sexuality in *Los recuerdos del porvenir* in the form of punishment, disappearance, and marginality is one of the motors of the novel, with sexual energy constantly threatening to erupt in the public and political realm. Yet even repressed, women's sexuality in Garro's novel is necessarily heterosexual. The single hint of lesbianism there is so explosive that it is immediately recuperated as asexual and self-referential. The twin sisters who share a bed so sensually also turn their soldier-abductor out of that bed, thus excising the sign of sexuality and power, the military phallus. The sisters are left to romp in innocence. The narrative world of received knowledge available to rural, isolated Ixtepec simply does not contain the possibility of lesbian sexuality, which is realizable only elsewhere, beyond Garro's text, as a metropolitan phenomenon, displaced, or dispersed, internationally.[1]

The nameless lesbian writer who is the protagonist of Sylvia Molloy's *En breve cárcel* (translated as *Certificate of Absence*) is an international traveler who takes refuge in the null space of exile that was so disconcerting in Gabriela Mistral and Cristina Peri Rossi.[2] Retreating into both herself and the claustrophobic space of her rented room, she undertakes the double process of reconnection to her alienated body and to the world. In contrast to the other texts under consideration in this study, Molloy's novel, written outside her native Argentina, struggles with its

96

acknowledgment of particular geographical spaces. *En breve cárcel* is a novel of the restoration of the lesbian body, in which the recognition and divulging of place becomes a synecdoche for self-disclosure and repair. As synecdoche it lends its fragmentary nature to its object: the protagonist's restoration is only partial. Though the place-names that locate her are ultimately written, her own name never is.

Both the writer's body and her room are sites of sexual knowledge and experience; they are the ground that makes the work of reconnection through writing possible. The protagonist's two identities, lesbian and writer, are intimately bound together, and her decision to withdraw into herself and her room to write is both chosen and imposed out of that double identity. The room she returns to for her writing, where she and each of her two lovers met and where those two women also became lovers, is simultaneously a solitary space and one with a history of formative relationships. The almost obsessive interiority of the novel can be read as both a consequence of and a metaphor for the repression of lesbianism, so that only within the self, the room, and the text she creates can the writer's lesbianism be represented as normative.

Like Alicia Partnoy, Molloy challenges the voyeuristic stance that has most often characterized the depiction of her subject. The *cárcel* (prison) of Molloy's title makes a literary trope of Partnoy's reality, but both texts take advantage of the narrow range of vision that prison imposes to direct the reader's gaze. Molloy's novel makes lesbianism visible, not as a function of male desire, but from a lesbian standpoint. Lesbian sexuality per se is unproblematic in the text. The writer's alienation from her body has to do with her own particular history, not with the fact of her sexuality.[3] In keeping with this achievement, my reading of *En breve cárcel* puts lesbianism at its center, so as not to reinscribe the silence that Molloy has broken. To gloss over the lesbianism in discussing the novel might be a way to claim the book's universality, but to say it is not "merely" a lesbian text would be analogous to criticism that claims Latin American writing for world literature, conveniently bypassing the cultural ground that provides it its particular character.[4]

The painful investigation of self that is the focus of Molloy's novel is an investigation of the lesbian body. The writer's project is the creation of a text that gives form and meaning to a body that, having already refused the heterosexual and heterosexist meanings others would ascribe to it, is culturally meaningless. This is the ground on which the novel is written, implicit in the text and crucial to it. In *En breve cárcel*, the text enables a recuperation of the body, made necessary by and in a sociosexual structure that disallows the female body for itself (*por sí* and *para sí*). The character's sexuality, not just her gender, is what most forcefully elucidates the dispossession of the body.

Molloy's text is political in its challenge of normative power relations around issues of women's sexuality, in its appropriation of the means of representation, and in its attentiveness to women's interactions with each other. The particular textualization of the lesbian body that Molloy's protagonist undertakes, however, is lesbian in its least political variation, and certainly not feminist. Feminism suggests some sort of interaction with societal structures—a political consciousness—which is thoroughly lacking in the protagonist of *En breve cárcel*. Here the protagonist/writer constructs her text in articulation with two other women, who have been both her and each other's lovers, and with her own past (where the emphasis on dreams suggests a Freudian, and, by extension, sexual, meaning to the past)—a very closed world. Molloy's character is not a feminist, or not discernibly so, even if the text lends itself to a feminist reading. Her relationships with other women have no apparent etiology—she is completely obsessed by her body, her writing, and her dreams; the relationships with her lovers are deliberately wrenched from any cultural context.[5] Her flight at the end of the novel is to no specific place, simply away from the places she has been before. Unlike the exiles discussed earlier, Molloy's protagonist betrays little regret at leaving those places that also, in fact, were sites of displacement for her.[6] When the world finally enters the novel—paradoxically, by means of the dreams that demand to be transcribed faithfully and therefore reveal the real-world place-names that connect the women back to the places they have inhabited—the writer's text comes to an end.

Body and Text

The human body is not just a physical phenomenon in the natural world; it is one of the most heavily burdened bearers of meaning in culture, and one of its richest sources of meaning derives from its gendered character. The meaning of the body-gendered-female is tied to an ideological structure of heterosexuality—women's bodies "mean" in relation to men's needs: nurturance, sex, physical care, a repository for human physicality when what men value is intellectual or spiritual. *En breve cárcel* takes as a focal point the relation between body and writing. Here, though, the body in question is not part of the heterosexual economy, but rather is in the process of forging new meanings. The text does not rehearse everything the writer's body is not—mother, wife, mistress, whore, celibate for God—but rather repeatedly lights on the uncharted and unbounded body. The text is so tightly focused, the room so claustrophobic, that unless we remember that we are readers reading and as such make the text meaningful in terms of the knowledge we bring to it, we can forget that outside the room the writer must walk in a heterosexual world. Her few forays into the street are brief and laden with anxiety. The decision to contain the body, to closet it as it were, functions as a textual strategy that permits the refusal of old meanings and offers the physical space in which the writer can risk formlessness in her search for form. The writer's body is not what the world expects it to be, but it is not yet anything else.[7]

Because there are no meanings "out there" already made that could be employed usefully to shape this body, it is in danger of collapsing. Moreover, since the lesbian body has been taken up by male heterosexual representation, usually in a pornographic or quasi-pornographic context where sexual relations between women are enacted for men, it is crucial to *make* meanings that prevent the lesbian body from being dismembered, or from being absorbed by heterosexist meanings, needs, and interpretations. By enclosing herself in her room, the protagonist of *En breve cárcel* shields herself from any such uninvited intrusion. The lesbianism of her text is normative to the extent that the heterosexual world is excluded; there is no place for the lascivious heterosexual male to stand. Just as the untenable viewpoint I expected to find in *The Little School* was disallowed, there is no space for a ringside seat to lesbian passion in *En breve cárcel*. Both texts narrow the range of vision to such an extreme that the way in which the reader can see is largely predetermined.

The writer can hope to reclaim her body only in a controlled space of this sort. Formless and always threatening to disintegrate, her body is, not surprisingly, foreign to her:

El cuerpo—su cuerpo—es de otro. Desconocimiento del cuerpo, contacto con el cuerpo, placer o violencia, no importa; el cuerpo es de otro. (31)

[The body—her body—belongs to someone else. Unfamiliarity with the body, contact with the body, pleasure or violence, all that does not matter: the body belongs to someone else. (18)]

Her childhood memories include no bodily memories, except as they refer to someone else. She has no recollection of pleasure, none of pain, and she only remembers her illnesses because they have been rendered textual: her parents told her the stories of her being born with a broken collarbone and of a serious childhood illness. What the writer recalls independently is not the sensation of pain or illness but the presence of her parents, that which is external to her, and which she both can and cannot differentiate from herself. Similarly, her efforts at control and containment begin with the more manageable task of mastering her surroundings when she herself threatens to go out of control. As a child she learned to keep sane by regulating her environment, making sure her room was in perfect order. Later, when she is ill, she makes her room neat, under control, before she gives in to sickness.

As an adult, illness, violence, and pain become ways to know the body. In a step toward wholeness, the writer has to acknowledge her own sick body—her mother is not there to do it for her. Science and society can confirm the illness (the thermometer shows she has fever; the concierge comments on the way she looks), but only after she recognizes the illness herself.[8] Once the writer has done this she deliberately exacerbates the distance between mind and body, alienating herself from her pain until the split is taken so far that mind and body must reconcile.

To push the body to its limits is to encounter her own boundaries, even to find out if they exist. In an invocation of her body's presence, the writer seeks pain:

Tambièn ella se ha dejado pegar, consciente. (33)

[She too has allowed herself to be beaten, fully conscious of what she was doing. (20)]

The writer also, with no little pleasure, inflicts pain: she invokes a childhood memory of hitting her sister with a belt. Pain inflicted on the sister is tantamount to pain inflicted on the self, however, since the writer comes closest to experiencing her own body as a child by observing the naked body of her sister. Looking at her own body, watching it age, is another form of violence:

A su cuerpo lo violenta, a solas, con la mirada. (34)

[When she is alone she violates her body by spying on it. (20)]

Nevertheless, her alienation from her body is so complete that often she doesn't even feel its pain:

Los tajos, las mutilaciones, son sin duda dolorosos pero está tan acostumbrada a las grietas, desde chica, que las imagina y aunque se las inflija deja de sentirlas. (35)

[Incisions, mutilations are no doubt painful, but since childhood she has gotten so used to imagining them that even when she inflicts them on herself she does not feel them. (21)]

The writer's self-assigned task is to construct a text that will hold the body that she feels is forever threatening to come apart. Early in the novel she remembers her lover Vera telling her, in French, that when they first met she looked uncomfortable in her skin. Skin remains an important motif:

Mal en su piel, mal de su piel, irritada con esa apariencia llena de fallas, de grietas. De chica le impresionaban mucho más que los esqueletos— que siempre le parecían cómicos—esos cuerpos que ilustran el sistema muscular en los diccionarios. (15-16)

[She is ill at ease in her skin and with her skin, annoyed by an appearance full of cracks and flaws. As a child she was less struck by pictures of skeletons (which always seemed comical to her) than by the illustrations of the muscular system she found in dictionaries. (5)]

She has repeated nightmares of skinlessness, of lack of boundaries and vulnerability.

Más de una vez ha soñado con despellejamientos, con su propio despellejamiento. Por ejemplo, se ha desdoblado, queda como una corteza pero no se ve, ve en cambio a un muchacho enfermo que tiene de la cintura para abajo el cuerpo despellejado, y a ella le ha tocado conservar la piel inútil de él. (16)

[More than once she has dreamed of flayings, of being flayed. For instance, she sees herself split: before her stands a sick boy, flayed from the waist down, while she is but a transparent peel. (5)]

She is "mal protegida por su piel ineficaz" (16) ["ill-protected by her in-effectual skin" (5)].[9]

Insofar as the culture's dominant discourse is taken on as one's own, it gives shape—meaning—to women's bodies both as external and self-generated constraint. This is the skin that the writer sheds.[10] Like Molloy, the French radical lesbian writer Monique Wittig removes the skin from the lesbian body, though in Wittig, the process is deliberate and erotic:

I discover that your skin can be lifted layer by layer, I pull it, it lifts off, it coils above your knees, I pull starting at the labia, it slides the length of the belly, fine to extreme transparency, I pull starting at the loins, the skin uncovers the round muscles and trapezii of the back, it peels off up to the nape of the neck, I arrive under your hair, m/y fingers traverse its thickness, I touch your skull, I grasp it with all my fingers, I press it, I gather the skin over the whole of the cranial vault, I tear off the skin brutally beneath the hair, I reveal the beauty of the shining bone traversed by blood vessels. . . .[11]

The removal of the skin becomes an act of love that opens the woman to her lover as it permits a new definition of self and body that includes the lover.

This peeling away of the skin causes the body to spill over, to flow outward. It is associated, in other words, with excess. Indeed, the writer's desire to gain control over her body, expressed throughout the text, is modulated by her desire to throw off restraint and exceed limits. Both these desires are informed by her sense that her body is alien to her. Giving the body over to pain is connected to her desire to defy limits:

En espejos enfrentados vio en una ocasión una de sus nalgas, surcadas de líneas rojas que interrumpían cada tanto los moretones dejados por una hebilla. Resultado de un encuentro más — y el último — con alguien que estaba decidido a sacarla de sí misma. (33)

[She once saw in a pair of mirrors how one of her buttocks was marked with red lines interrupted every so often by the bruises left by a buckle. Results of one more meeting — the last — with someone who had decided to draw her out of herself. (20)]

This sort of sexual excess is what the writer values in Renata, the lover whose absence is the generating factor in the text:

Con Renata ha vivido — como no con Vera — la falta de límites, ha compartido un lugar (que ahora se le antoja este lugar, donde escribe) donde todo le parecía posible, donde cabía el exceso: gritos, gestos, exageraciones, violencia, todo lo que sintió como vedado. (27)

[Life with Renata (not with Vera) implied a lack of limits. With her she has shared a space (which she now associates with this room where she is writing) where everything seemed possible, where even the excessive had its place: shouts, gestures, exaggeration, violence, everything that she felt had always been denied her. (15)]

Space here is no longer just the physically measurable dimensions of the room, but the morally and culturally unbounded mental/spiritual/sexual space of particular acts. "This room where she is writing" has become the literary space she is forging for this text as well as the limited environment she can keep more or less under control.[12]

Simultaneous with her desire for the order imposed by narration is the writer's urge to break out of that which confines her. Significantly, the novel's only explicit scene of sexual intimacy represents both the defiance of limits and their imposition. Renata's insistence that the writer remain standing during the encounter is a restriction of her movements, but the pleasure, humiliation, and muted violence of the lovemaking are forms of excess.

Ultimately, the old skin (which in this text has already been peeled away, if not entirely shed) must be replaced by new. Not surprisingly, the act of writing is repeatedly figured in *En breve cárcel* as the creation of an organic, self-generated cover. The pages of the text become like layers of skin, or scales—text as a bodily secretion that contains, protects, and gives form to the body. The narrator struggles to find this metaphor and offers it up with no little sense of accomplishment:

> Una clave, un orden para este relato. Sólo atina a ver capas, estratos, como en los segmentos de la corteza terrestre que proponen los manuales ilustrados. No: como las diversas capas de piel que cubren músculos y huesos, imbricadas, en desapacible contacto. Estrecimiento, erizamiento de la superficie: ¿quién no ha observado, de chico, la superficie interior de una costra arrancada y la correspondiente llaga rosada, sin temblar? En ese desgarramiento inquisidor se encuentran clave y orden de esta historia. (23)

> [A key, an ordering principle for this story. She can see only layers, strata, as in the segments of the earth's crust shown in schoolbooks. No, more like the various layers of skin that cover muscles and bones, overlapping, in unpleasant contact. Quivering, bristling surfaces. Who has not observed as a child, after pulling off a scab, the inner surface and the pink sore that goes with it—and looked at it without trembling? In that inquisitive act of destruction she finds the key and ordering principle for this story. (12)]

The strands the writer is pulling together (the story of Vera, the story of Renata, the story of her childhood) might in the end weave themselves together to reveal, "como las capas de piel en el libro de anatomía, el sistema de su imbricación" (24) ["like the layers of skin in the anatomy book, how they are connected to one another" (12)]. On the other hand, these stories might not join together in a coherent text after all. Language holds no easy promise for the writer, since it figures so prominently in the cultural system that has produced the bodily configuration she refuses.

Molloy rings numerous variations on the theme of verbal representation in connection with sensuality and the generation of skin.[13] The story that Vera, the writer's lover, tells is "[un] relato que se deleitaba en sí mismo, piel que había logrado componer" (22) ["a story that took delight in itself, like a tight skin Vera had managed to smooth" (10)]. Later, during a reverie both produced and captured in a session of free writing, the writer's words take on a floating corporeality and attach themselves to her body:

> Ve que las palabras se levantan una vez más, como se levanta ella, agradece la letra ondulante que la enlaza, reconoce las cicatrices en un cuerpo que acaricia. Vuelven a romperse cuerpo y frase, pero no en la misma cicatriz: se abren de manera distinta, le ofrecen una nueva fisura que esta tarde acepta, en la que no ve una violencia mala, en la que sospecha un orden. (67)

> [The words arise once more, as she herself rises. She is thankful for those undulating words that hold her again, caressing her body and recognizing her scars. Her body and her phrase will tear again, but not at the old scars: they will split open in a different way, revealing new fractures. She accepts this future violence as something not necessarily negative, as a sign, perhaps, of a secret order. (48)]

Still another version of the text as secretion is writing as exorcism, expelling the words so they no longer poison from within:

> Lo que escribe es una manera de ir tachando para seguir adelante. (139)

> [Writing is really a form of erasure in order to keep going. (108-9)]

At one point the writer connects the completion of her task with death:

> Se pregunta si es miedo o impotencia, si teme morirse escribiendo— incrustar una anécdota y luego desaparecer. (20)

> [She wonders if it is fear or impotence, whether she is afraid of dying while she writes (of disappearing after casting [Spanish: encrusting] a story). (9)]

But what dies at the end of the novel is the possibility of any future relationship with Renata or Vera. Once the skin or scab or shell is cast, the text made material, the writer goes away, leaving the text behind even as she takes it with her. The snoopy narrator, who doggedly records the

writer's writing, retains her text—the one we read—while the writer flies
off hugging the sheets of her manuscript to her:

> Ha decidido armarse para el ejercicio: no hay alcohol, ni droga, ni
> tabaco que la ayuden. . . . Desamparada, se aferra a las páginas que ha
> escrito para no perderlas. (158)

> [She has decided to ready herself (Spanish: *armarse*: arm herself, put on
> armor) for the test. There is no alcohol, no drug, no tobacco to help her.
> . . . Unprotected, she clings to the pages she has written so as not to lose
> them. (125)]

Through words/texts/pages/voice the writer longs to order and delin-
eate, create the boundaries between the pleasures of writing, sex, and
dreams. She will create order out of the chaos of events that touch her
day:

> Escribe hoy lo que hizo, lo que no hizo, para verificar fragmentos de un
> todo que se le escapa. Cree recuperarlos, con ellos intenta—o inventa—
> una constelación suya. (13)

> [Today she is writing down what she has done, what she has not done,
> trying to grasp the fragments of a whole that escapes her. She believes
> she can recover them, and with them tries to make—or make up—her
> own private constellation. (3)]

She chooses in her writing to make a form that will contain and order
chaos.

In a recuperative move, skin becomes a product of voice, and voice is
associated with health:

> En cambio no se ve sin voz (como no se ve sin piel) y acaso el riesgo de
> esa imaginación sea su mayor amenaza: reconoce la salud, se aferra a
> ella, en términos de una entonación. Algo, la voz ronca de su tía, la voz
> cascada de Renata, su propia voz cuando escribe, algo, una piel de
> voces, para entonar los fragmentos. (35)

> [On the other hand she cannot imagine herself without a voice, just as
> she cannot imagine herself without a skin. The mere thought is in itself
> threatening: she identifies health (and clings to it, as it were) with the
> intonations of a voice. Some voice, the hoarse voice of her aunt,
> Renata's husky voice, or her own voice when she writes: a skin of voices
> to give shape to (Spanish: *entonar*: to shape, tune, tone) these fragments.
> (21)]

Here the writer combines the fear of being without skin—vulnerable and raw—with the surety of always having a voice. "She cannot imagine herself without" in one case denotes the fear of losing—skin; in the other, the knowledge of having—voice. They come together at the end of the paragraph when her own writerly voice meshes with the voices of her aunt and her lover, transformed into a skin that tunes the fragments. *Entonar*, with its aural connotations of music, also carries the meaning of harmonize or modulate, to bring together the disparate pieces of the fragmented self into a coherent whole. Its reflexive meaning is also recalled: "to strengthen the muscular fibers by means of tonic medicine." Skin (or, more precisely, its equivalent) and voice are further equated in a pleasurable way: Vera's voice is like the sleeve of her black velvet jacket.

Neither Molloy nor her writer is "writing the body," but rather spinning it a protective covering—weaving a skin, creating order, giving shape. Feminists have called this naming, coming out, finding a voice. When she has completed the text, the writer emerges from her room/cocoon, which had been a temporary and only partially protective covering, and she is no longer vulnerable and formless, but rather defiant, clad in the text she spun out of her need. Lest this seem an overly optimistic ending, we are reminded that her fear remains, though she now can be in the world despite it.

Although the production of the text is, finally, a healthy act, it is not without its difficulties and perils. The first chapter of the novel can be read paradoxically, as the avoidance of storytelling:

> Hoy no quiere hablar más de Vera, no quiere extrañar más a Renata. . . . Desvía una narración, se dice que la dilata para contarla mejor; por fin la posterga porque no la puede contar. Quisiera que estos trozos de relato fueran como los cuentos de Vera, mejores que los cuentos de Vera: imperturbables. Pero teme anotarlos porque sabe muy bien que le duele mucho contar esta historia. (24-25)

> [Today she does not want to say any more about Vera, does not want to miss Renata anymore. . . . She deflects a narrative, telling herself she puts it off in order to tell it better. Ultimately, however, she postpones it because she cannot tell it. She wishes these scraps of fiction were like Vera's anecdotes, or even better than Vera's anecdotes: impassive. But she is afraid to write them down because she knows very well how much it hurts to tell this story. (13)]

To tell the story of the avoidance of storytelling is also to engage in storytelling; and the loss of the lover, Renata, is doubly the occasion for the text. If Renata had kept her date with the writer, there would be neither the story of her not coming nor the time to write it. During the painful wait for Renata, who will not arrive, the protagonist constitutes herself as writer, and Renata's very absence from the room effects her presence in the text. In perhaps the only truly amusing moment in the novel, Renata, having learned that her ex-lover is writing a book, pays her a visit, behaves perfectly charmingly, and rewrites a little of their personal history so that she will come off well as a character.

Both Renata and the writer know that stories can harm. Renata tells gratuitous lies that fail to hide her infidelities, and the writer elaborates tales of infidelity with which to wound her lover. Vera is also a storyteller who uses her sad tales of betrayal to seduce and control potential and actual lovers. Moreover, the writer hates the idea that Renata has probably turned her into an anecdote with which to entertain her current lover.

The distinction between spoken and written stories is also a factor here. Because it feels like a breach of confidence, the writer does not repeat Vera's childhood story to her hosts—but she goes home and writes it down into this narrative. Spoken texts too easily harm; written ones are healing. In the end, though, writing and speech converge in the desire for communication. The writer wants to write a spoken language as Renata sleeps, to declare her love for Renata:

> Renata duerme y ella quiere escribir, una vez más, en este cuarto. Decir que la quiere a Renata, decirle—me haces falta. Decirle: Renata, yo estoy en tu cuerpo y por tu cuerpo, como por el mío hablo. . . . Pero Renata duerme. (157)

> [Renata is asleep and she wants to write, one more time, in this room. She would like to say that she loves Renata, to say: I need you. She would like to say: Renata, I am in your body and speak through your body as well as through my own. . . . But Renata is asleep. (124)]

What she longs for here is an integration of writing and speech, a way to express the integration of herself and this lover, to write a spoken declaration of love. The narrator then backs up and shows us that she *has* been writing (this?): "Deja de escribir" (157) ["She stops writing" (124)]. Paradoxically, she can write but cannot speak, and both because Renata is asleep.

Geography

The dialectical relation between containment and excess played out in terms of the writer's body is echoed in the treatment of geographical space in the novel. Whereas the exile writers discussed in chapter 3 clearly knew where they were leaving from, part of this character's task is to discover the meaning of the places she had been before. Her text establishes a relationship between place and self that it simultaneously works to suppress in the struggle to tell a story that is new and dangerous. The observation that "Para viajar es necesario saber de dónde se parte" (148) ["to travel one needs to know where one is leaving from" (117)] expresses the writer's conflicted desire to know where she was in order to know where she is going, for that is not only information about place, but also about self. That link is elsewhere figured more overtly in the atypical grammar of "Soy donde fui—o donde no fui, soy donde seré" (148), where the adverb of place wrests new meaning from the verb: "I am the place I was— or the place I was not, I am the place I will be" (my translation; differently in Balderston, 117).

The writer is a traveler who moves between three continents, yet with few exceptions such action as there is in this text takes place in tightly enclosed spaces. Furthermore, the issue of language is suppressed—it is implied that the writer speaks English with Renata and French with Vera. Although language may not signal changes in meaning for the writer, it does to Molloy. She worked closely with Balderston on the translation of the novel, so where the English version departs from the original it does so with her blessing. The novel's two titles, for example, have roots deep in each language's culture as lines of poetry, and each evokes a different aspect of the text. "En breve cárcel," from a poem by the Spanish baroque poet Francisco de Quevedo, refers to the frame encircling the miniature portrait of the speaker that the lover carries. Likening love to that "small prison" binding the lover, the Spanish phrase evokes the enclosure and claustrophobia of the novel. "Certificate of Absence" comes from an Emily Dickinson poem and points to the freedom afforded by anonymity. It recalls Dickinson's more famous "I'm nobody," but with the paradoxical license provided by anonymity foregrounded and, with the naming of the "certificate," ironically given something like official and public sanction.

Geography in this novel is a puzzle for the reader and a problem for the writer. Fictional and actual space are in constant tension, and the de-

sire to name places, attaching them to a reality external to both the writer's text and the novel, is repeatedly invoked and deferred. The writer experiments with various means of evoking place, using techniques that the
narrator characterizes as a kind of flirtation. The sexually nuanced term
is intriguing in this context, since part of the reason for suppressing the
names of the cities is to forge a new and separate lesbian space:

> Querría describirla, evocar el primer encuentro hace cuatro años en casa
> de Vera, en pleno centro de aquella ciudad sofocada por la nieve.
> Ciudad que no nombra por ahora, que acaso no nombre: en cada nueva
> copia de este texto propone geografías vagas, una latitud frígida
> aceptable, un invento nevado que no la convence, que tacha. Querría no
> nombrar, por coquetería, con desenfado. Sabe que nombrar es un rito,
> ni más ni menos importante que la inscripción de una frase trivial. Pero
> también sabe que los nombres, las iniciales que había escrito en una
> primera versión, han sido sustituidos; la máscara del nombre que
> recuerda, del nombre con que dijo, con que creyó que decía, ha sido
> reemplazada por otra, más satisfactoria porque más lejana. Se pregunta
> por qué disimula nombres literalmente insignificantes cuando pretende
> transcribir, con saña, una realidad vivida. (19)

> [She would like to describe her, to evoke their first meeting four years
> ago at Vera's house, downtown in that city smothered in snow. A city
> she will not name for now, that she will perhaps never name; each new
> version of this text suggests vague topographies, a suitably bleak
> latitude, a snowy fiction she finds unconvincing and scratches out.
> Coquettishly, recklessly, she chooses not to name. She knows that to
> name is a ritual, neither more nor less important than the recording of a
> trivial sentence. But she also knows that the names, the initials she had
> included in an earlier version of this story have been replaced by others;
> the mask of the name she remembers, of the name she uttered or
> thought she uttered, has been changed to another one, more satisfactory
> because more distant. She asks herself why she conceals names that are
> insignificant while at the same time trying furiously to transcribe a lived
> reality. (8)]

Barely ten pages before the end of the novel the narrator, following the
writer's decision, finally reveals the external geography of the novel.

> En estos sueños que sin cesar la hacen visitar ciudades—Amberes, París,
> Roma, Buenos Aires—donde con su madre, donde con su hermana,
> recorre espacios sin saber adónde va. En todas hay un punto secreto y
> ella no lo encuentra.
> Ha tenido que mencionar nombres de ciudades. Esto la molesta, pero
> son parte de sus sueños. La ciudad nevada donde conoció a Renata y

volvió a ver a Vera es la ciudad de Buffalo, en el estado de Nueva York. La ciudad donde volvió a encontrar a Renata y Vera es París. Y la ciudad donde creció y—si le dieran la elección—volvería a crecer, es la ciudad de Buenos Aires. (147)

[There is something . . . in these dreams and in many others like them, dreams that have her continuously leading her mother and sister through cities—Antwerp, Paris, Rome, Buenos Aires—without knowing where she is going. In all of them there is a secret point she never finds.

She has had to mention the names of cities. This troubles her, but they are after all part of her dreams. She now decides to give places—all her places—their name. The snowy city where she met Renata and spied on Vera again is Buffalo, New York. The city where she met up again with Renata and Vera is Paris. The city where she grew up—and where she would grow up again, given the choice—is the city of Buenos Aires. (116)]

Once the cities have made their way into her dreams, the writer concludes that as part of her internal landscape they must be revealed. Usable reality is generated from within, and the outside world can be permitted to emerge only when assimilated and reproduced internally. Also, it is only fair that the writer reveal the cities' names to the astute reader who has read the clues along the way, hypothesized about the real-world locations of those places, and deserves the reward of finding out if these conclusions were correct.[14] Telling also serves a psychological cause: to protect the writer.

Ha dado claves, se siente tranquila. Pero sabe que ha caído en estas revelaciones tardías para no seguir enfrentándose con presencias femeninas, para protegerse de ellas. (147)

[She has pointed out clues, and now feels at peace. She is aware, however, that she has fallen into these tardy revelations so as not to go on facing those feminine presences, to protect herself from them. (116)]

Designating a real geography engulfs the women in meanings extant in those places and summons the preexisting definitions of relationships, body, texts that the writer has been working, painfully, to undo and remake. Simultaneously, though, the power of her mother, sister, and lovers to descend upon the writer as terrifying presenses is defused once these figures are released into real geography.[15]

The cities that press their meanings onto the characters are rendered usable when they become dream spaces that at least contain the promise of new meaning, even if the writer cannot yet grasp it:

En todas hay un punto secreto y ella no lo encuentra. (147)

[In all of them is a secret point she never finds. (116)]

Real geography, in the company of the mother and the sister, can, potentially, be transformed. The mythical geography with which her father exhorts her, on the other hand, is static, and is ultimately rejected.

The internalized voice of the dead father tells the writer to go to the shrine of the fertility goddess, Artemis, the other aspect of Diana the virgin huntress, to whom the writer is drawn. The geography of this dream is unlike the other geography of the novel since in a material sense it is not anywhere. It only exists as a cultural imperative, the father's exhortation to the daughter to worship at the shrine of heterosexuality and conventional motherhood.

> Sabe que al decirle Efeso está rompiendo la geografía apenas nombrada de este relato para llamarle la atención sobre un lugar único al que nunca podrá llegar. (153)
>
> [She realizes that, in saying the word Ephesus, her father was altering the almost nameless geography of her story, calling attention to the only place she would never be able to reach. (121)]

The temple of Artemis on Ephesus was burned down the night Alexander the Great was born. There is literally no way to go there. What her father wants is for her to return to a heterosexual mythology that no longer exists.[16]

Mapmaking

The most obvious geographical question this novel presents is, why Buffalo? Virtually everybody writes between Paris and Buenos Aires: that particular dislocation is an all but canonical trope in Argentine literature. But Buffalo? Since Molloy does not exploit the local color (except as shades of white and gray, the colors of snow), the only explanation that makes sense is that *En breve cárcel* is to some extent autobiographical. Though we cannot assert the autobiographical nature of the novel without going outside the book itself, the book's ancillary texts — the author's biographical note and the jacket copy — reveal that the geography of the novel is congruent with Molloy's personal geography.[17]

Molloy plays with the autobiographical mode (her narrator reports on a writer who is piecing together the contours of a textual self), but she knows enough about autobiography as a genre to know that what her writer is writing is not an autobiography.[18] Instead, her text "tries to reproduce a disjointed series of acts of violence" that have touched her and others (49) ["Querrían componer una serie de violencias salteadas" (68)]. The writer's text lacks both a sustained narrative and a focus on an individuated self, and in particular avoids the single most important characteristic of Spanish American autobiography identified by Molloy herself, to wit, the subject's desire to be representative: "The Spanish American 'I' (if one dare generalize in this fashion) seems to rely more than other 'I's' — to rely in a nearly ontological manner — on a sort of national recognition. Representativity and identity are closely linked in Spanish American self-writing."[19] Molloy's writer not only eschews any sense of representativity; she hides her geographical origins until the very end, so that she ostensibly cannot even have representativity thrust upon her. Of course the disenfranchised lesbian is not likely to constitute herself as representative of her culture or even of her sex as, say, Victoria Ocampo did.[20]

Since she reads the writer's text in order to fashion her own, the narrator of *En breve cárcel* is connected to the reader as well as to the writer. The narrator has access to the writer's written words, the texts that she produces — including the writing she does in the room waiting for Renata and the already transcribed dreams she keeps in a folder left over from when she was a student. The narrator, like the writer (and the author), is also a reader of texts and an explorer of the writing process.

I have been deliberate in calling Molloy's protagonist "the writer," both because that is what she is, and because the term constantly threatens to refer to Molloy herself. *En breve cárcel* not only represents women writing, but it places the author, narrator, and protagonist in uncomfortably close proximity. Events get reported with very little lag time — barely enough to see that there are events that are being edited out of what the writer is writing, not just by the writer but by the voice narrating her as well. At times it seems that the writer is just one draft ahead of the narrator. The space is so claustrophobic that there seems to be no place for the narrator to be *but* in the room with the writer. The relationship between the narrator and the writer is like the relationship between the writer and the other women characters. They are not conflated, but neither are they totally separable. They are bound to each other, similarly situated in the world (women writing/women loving women/beings with women's bodies), and their position in the universe depends on their relationship to each other. "Writer," "author," and "narrator" are all aspects of the text-producing function. In this text, the narrator mediates between the author, embodied in the world outside the text, and the writer/protagonist, evoked on the page, within the text. Nothing is revealed of the narrator, but the author's life bears striking resemblance, in at least some of its aspects, to the character's.

In *En breve cárcel* there is no individuated self. The writer does not break free of the others (Vera, Renata, mother, and sister)—she incorporates them into her text, which is the shape she gives her self. The defining of a self through relationships with others is a frightening notion to a male writer-friend of hers, whose self is created through rigid boundaries separating him from "the other," and who wants his text to stand alone and bounded. For her, however, the idea of being a self in process and in relation is liberating.

> El tiene miedo, rechaza la idea de que la novela que ha escrito integre la realidad no como objeto sino como relación vivida. Cuando lo oyó hablar se sintió tocada, se dio cuenta de que ella también corteja un espacio intermedio: reconoce que al transcribir ordena y se permite cambiar nombres pero pretende dilucidar, en un plano que sabe de antemano inseguro, un episodio cuyas posibilidades ignora, cuyos antecedentes fluctúan, y que querría definitivo. (20)

> [He is upset, rejecting the idea that the novel he has written has become a part of reality, not as an object but as a lived experience. As he speaks, she identifies with what he is saying, realizing that she too courts ambiguity. She recognizes that she imposes her own order on what she transcribes, permitting herself to change a few names, but at the same time tries, on another level (courting danger, she knows), to discover what really happened: in spite of the unknown possibilities, in spite of the shifting past, she would like the story to be definitive. (8)]

Though the promise of fixity is tempting, she knows she seeks that intermediate space between chaos and control.[21]

At the end of the novel, closed in on by the women she loves (mother, sister, Renata, Vera), the writer declares that she bade them come. But she corrects herself: she does not decide imperiously when and if they should appear, it is that she needs them. These women have never been completely separable from her or from each other, but now she recognizes that they form a whole; and together they achieve the recuperation of a past that gets beyond the father. The writer's bonds with Vera and Renata—whose names suggest truth and rebirth—enable her to dream

the not-so-buried female past of mother and sister and exorcize the incestuous dream of the father.

Molloy's problematization of the relationship between author/writer
and protagonist/writer is another door out of the novel's room. The latter's text may never be published, read, and discussed, but the former's
has been. *En breve cárcel* is not autobiography, but it entwines with autobiography in such a way that Molloy's novel, if not the text its protagonist is writing, comes back to the production of communal reality. As
Molloy demonstrates elsewhere, to represent the self is also, for Latin
American autobiographers, to represent the community.[22] Just as Alicia
Partnoy counters what was the official silence concerning the Dirty War
in Argentina, and Gaby Brimmer claims her presence as part of Mexican
reality, *En breve cárcel* makes claims on Latin American reality for the
presence of lesbianism, even if it must go elsewhere to name itself. The
"certificate of absence" of the English title of this novel was invented by
a poet who is increasingly read as a lesbian writer. Like the novel itself,
Emily Dickinson's phrase plays on the notion of presence in absence, already linked to the phenomenon of exile, and which also applies to the
lesbian. Beyond range of the sight lines of the law of the father, the lesbian is not "seen" on her own terms, but she *is* in danger of being otherwise apprehended. Exile provides the protective cape of invisibility, another layer of absence, to the lawbreaker. Molloy's protagonist's double
exile from her country and from the outside world is, as far as the reader
can tell, self-imposed. Her room is the no-place of the exile discussed in
chapter 3, though deliberately chosen and haunted by other absences. I
resist calling her lesbianism another exile, because the metaphor has been
so overused by feminist literary scholars that it threatens to erase the literal exile from one's country that has so deeply marked the Latin American experience. Here, as in the earlier chapter, an exile that is not coter-
minous with femininity or lesbianism may be the only place where the
lesbian can find herself and be found, and the mediation of a sympathetic
feminist reading may facilitate bringing her back home.

8

Cristina Peri Rossi and the
Question of Lesbian Presence

I return to Cristina Peri Rossi in this chapter to address the intersection
of politics, gender, and sexuality that I have argued must be the crux
of a Latin American feminist criticism, and also to confront the irony
that in any individual text by Peri Rossi these elements rarely meet
head-on. Though she has stated that she considers sexual freedom and
the end of class and gender oppression as part of the same revolutionary
agenda it would be a mistake to assume that when Peri Rossi deals
with gender, or lesbianism, or class, or colonialism she invokes them all.[1]
Instead, Peri Rossi masks the connections among these sites of oppression. Claiming that she tends not to consider all of her concerns in any
one text, instead "compensating" in one for what was underrepresented
in the last, or by deliberately contrasting her erotic poetry to her politically committed texts, she allows the reader to cling to narrowly political
or aesthetic discussions of her work and to ignore its lesbian content,
simply by concentrating on those texts where that content is least
visible.

Certain of Peri Rossi's poems and stories are lesbian in content, but
many are not, and one might be a respectful and serious reader of her
work without much taking into account that content, perhaps after acknowledging it. In fact, most of the criticism of Peri Rossi's writing, including my discussion of her work in chapter 3, does just that. It is not

coincidental that Peri Rossi is regarded as a mainstream writer and that a silence surrounds her lesbian voice.[2]

I want to think here about what it means to call Cristina Peri Rossi a "lesbian writer" and her work "lesbian writing." "Lesbian writer" is a term, like "woman writer," "exile writer," or "Latin American writer," whose primary function seems to be to categorize the writing subject, but which is invoked because it has something to say about her texts. Because these terms have important cultural meaning, they are assumed to make an interesting difference in literary production. Unlike the other terms, which have become legitimate if not uncontested, however, the label "lesbian writer" is still highly charged. Furthermore, "exile" and "Latin American," and even "woman," are readily verifiable categories, but to apply the adjective "lesbian" often means to rely on a combination of textual evidence and biographical intimation. In Peri Rossi's case, a few highly mediated interviews ambiguously suggest the writer's lesbian sexuality, and virtually none of the criticism of her work pays attention to lesbian textuality. The adjective "lesbian" gestures primarily toward the writer herself in large part because critics of Latin American literature have not thought of it as textually meaningful.

Does the fact that Peri Rossi has written a few texts that celebrate lesbian sexuality mean that we want to read everything she has written with that in mind? Do her overtly lesbian texts enrich and inform the rest? Certainly Peri Rossi's early male-voiced erotic poems need to be reread in the light of her later, openly lesbian work and of her own claim that those early poems are "homosexual."[3] But what is a lesbian critical stance toward a text when the theme is not love or sex, when traditional characterization disappears, when plot is minimized, when everything we attach to identity is disattached? What, in fact, is lesbian literature? Though it is certainly not simply the representation of sexuality by and for lesbians, in the United States lesbian literature has been easiest to recognize when there has been a confluence of lesbian writers, lesbian readers, and a text that deals with lesbian matters. But for writers who are (probably) lesbians, and who write (sometimes) about lesbianism, and who are given heterosexist readings, the ground gets muddy.[4]

The desire to codify lesbian experience for a lesbian audience in the United States comes out of a tradition that values individual identity, a tradition that has by now been redesigned so that the body of the individual is as highly valued as the mind that has been abstracted from it. But this revaluing does not question the notion of the bounded self as the basis for a unitary identity. Much of Peri Rossi's work, on the other hand, represents the fragmented self in exile, and her political culture posits an ideal identity that is collective.

The corpus of Cristina Peri Rossi's writing resists any totalizing classification. Despite the fact that *I* want a way to read her that takes into account her politics, her sexuality, her working-class background, her life as a Uruguayan in exile and as a theorist of literature as well as a writer of it, this simply may not be possible. An all-encompassing theory based on a mathematical model of elegant simplicity may be an unachievable goal. This is troubling because although feminist criticism has made a good case for the open-ended, incomplete, even internally contradictory text—the unresolved and unresolvable difference within, to use Elizabeth Abel's phrase—there remains an impulse toward stable identity (the textual version of which is the coherent text or corpus) as a foundation of identity politics. To be identifiable as a lesbian or a politically committed individual has meant to be identified in that oppositional position and (watch as we enter into the precarious land of prescription) to carry that identity through in all one's acts, including leaving important traces of such identity in the text. Peri Rossi, though, does not unfurl all her identities or all her concerns in each of her texts, claiming that each of her books answers the previous one, taking up in one what she has left out of the last. Moreover, Peri Rossi often deliberately effaces herself in what she writes.

Yet an oppositional identification underlies the *authenticity* of the text, which for political Latin American writers, as for North American lesbian writers, is essential. I read Peri Rossi as if she were a lesbian, even though I do not know for certain that she is. In her many interviews she speaks sympathetically of lesbianism and talks about the homosexuality [*sic*] in many of her texts, but to my knowledge she has never said publically, "As a lesbian I . . . " For me, however, as a feminist reader for whom the text is always contextual, it is vital to be able to place the author. The fact that Peri Rossi was politically active and had to go into exile adds depth and value to her fictional and poetic accounts of these issues. For writers who identify with some form of protest against the norm, literature is radically connected to knowledge and to social change. This is not a matter of "truth" or naive assumptions about the transparency of language. Politically astute subordinate groups are keenly aware of how control of language is a power issue, that the power to name is the power to call something into being and to evaluate it for others. Inventing an appropriate, authentic language is a key issue for lesbian and Latin American literature alike. Authenticity in this context comes not from a self-knowing and self-representing bounded individuality, but rather from another notion of the self that is both fragmented and part of a collectivity.

Peri Rossi asserts that poetry is not about individual identity but about a worldview, linked to a shared political reality:

> Durante mucho tiempo nos hemos refugiado en definir a la poesía como "otra cosa," oscura, inclasificable, algo que pertenece al reino de lo misterioso e irracional; relegarla a ese ámbito ha sido una forma de marginarla de los circuitos habituales del lector de la crítica, de las editoriales y de los medios de difusión. Enrarecida, aislada, abandonada como visión del mundo (para ser, casi siempre, visión del yo del poeta) casi nadie la ha buscado como lo que es, forma de conocimiento, de interpretación, de imagen del universo. (63)

> [For a long time we have taken refuge in defining poetry as "something else," dark, unclassifiable, something that belongs to the reign of the mysterious and irrational. Relegating it to this realm has been a way of marginalizing it from the habitual circuits of the reader of criticism, from publishing houses, and from the means of distribution. Rarified, isolated, abandoned as a vision of the world (in order to become, almost always, a vision of the I of the poet), almost no one has wanted it for what it is, a kind of knowledge, of interpretation, of image of the universe.][5]

This concept of poetry's broader scope is born of a notion of society far different from the bourgeois individualism of the United States. For Peri Rossi, the self is not isolated, and that which touches one profoundly is not limited to what occurs only in one's own mind and body. Social and political issues do not take the place of the self in Peri Rossi's poems, making them abstract, cold propaganda pieces. On the contrary, these concerns enrich the self, locating it in a community at risk that cannot be taken for granted. The poem, then, becomes more profoundly human, multidimensional and textured. Technical and aesthetic questions such as the nature of language and of poetry, political questions such as the military takeover of a country and the effects of that on its people, and intimate and personal questions such as sexuality, love, and memory, are all in play.

Such intimacy does not necessarily imply autobiography, however. In the same essay I just cited, Peri Rossi asserts that the speaker is identified with the poet in only two poems of *Europa después de la lluvia* (Europe after the rain).[6] Both poems have to do primarily with loss and exile, and with the resultant sense of déjà vu. Neither is specific as to the gender of the speaker, but both speak to a common experience of the exile.[7] The poet does associate herself with the speaker of the poems of *Evohé*, her first book of poetry, a book that, as she expected, scandalized those readers who had come to know her as a politically committed writer. In an interview with John Deredita, Peri Rossi says:

> El lector politizado (o sea, todos los lectores del país) estaba acostumbrado a encontrar en mi narrativa una alegoría, una metáfora que siempre tenía un nivel político, larvario o muy elaborado. . . . Es posible que en ese momento de intensa lucha política, de guerra interna declarada por el gobierno contra la subversión (y ya sabemos todo lo que suele englobar esa palabra fascista), y luego de poemas sociales y políticos que yo había publicado en diarios y revistas, la índole de *Evohé*, libro erótico y homosexual, causara mucha sorpresa. Yo contaba con ese factor, y pienso que no fue una actitud de desafío . . . lo que me hizo publicarlo, sino el deseo de establecer la necesidad de seguir viviendo, aun en medio de la guerra, de seguir creando y de reflexionar sobre la naturaleza del amor y de la escritura aun cuando se escuchan los tiros. (134)

> [The politicized reader (i.e., all the readers in the country) was used to finding in my narrative an allegory, a metaphor that always had a political level, larval or highly elaborated. . . . It is possible that in that moment of intense political struggle, of internal war declared by the government against subversion (and we all know what that fascist term tends to cover), and after the social and political poems that I had published in several newspapers and magazines, the nature of *Evohé*, an erotic and homosexual book, could have caused a good deal of surprise. I expected that factor, and I think that it was not an attitude of defiance . . . that made me publish it, but rather the desire to establish the need to keep living, even in the middle of the war, to keep creating and to reflect on the nature of love and writing even when you can hear the bullets.][8]

Here Peri Rossi identifies with the speaker of her poems simply by saying that the poems are homosexual. That she considered *Evohé* to be lesbian poetry even though the speaker is male suggests that we are to remain conscious of the woman's hand writing the poems. Peri Rossi is deliberately, even playfully, ambiguous with sexual meanings. Elsewhere in this interview she disingenuously suggests that the reason she wrote the poems of *Evohé* with a female erotic object was because the conventions were already in place, as if her use of them did not profoundly challenge those conventions. Peri Rossi makes it easy enough to read *Evohé* as a lesbian work, citing Sappho at the beginning and informing her readers that *Evohé* is the erotic cry of women celebrants in the rites of Dionysus.

The contradictions and ambiguities inherent in Peri Rossi's presentation of sexuality need to be taken at face value. Though not unproblematic, they are deliberate: part of Peri Rossi's project is to shake loose the rigidity of existing gender categories.

Heterosexism makes sexuality the sine qua non of gender identification. A "real woman" enjoys pleasing men sexually, is a devoted mother. A "real man" takes his pleasure from women and leaves a trail of children behind him. When feminist theory offers its most far-reaching insight— that gender is a primary category of analysis—on some level it engages the traditional means of distinguishing men from women and the masculine from the feminine. Though feminism calls into question gender so construed, feminist analysis still relies on the stability of some form of gender differentiation that has some connection to sex.[9] Peri Rossi returns to the underpinnings in sexuality of gender differentiation (which have not been contested in Latin America) to undermine heterosexist readings of gender. That is to say, insofar as gender classification remains chained to sexuality, Peri Rossi escapes the constraints of gender by refusing heterosexuality.

This strategy is one of two possible ways of loosening the binds of gender, though it is not the one most North American feminists have chosen. In the United States, we see, rather, a reform of gender categories. North American feminists have tended to do this by claiming that gender is culturally constructed and then attempting to reconstruct it by replacing rigid prescriptions of gender-appropriate behavior and the devaluation of women with more flexible, individually elaborated notions of what women and men can (rather than should) do, and a positive valuation of even traditional feminine characteristics. Peri Rossi, coming from a culture where this loosening has hardly begun, retains the rigidity of gender polarity and especially its connection to norms of heterosexuality, the better to shatter it. Especially in her early writings, Peri Rossi lacks a lesbian feminist community that, to quote two U.S. lesbian visual artists, "creates a new space for freedom of thought, fantasy, and scale which allows for the creation of a lesbian art dealing with lesbianism as everything that is possible—a woman-centered world view—rather than being limited by the constrictions of a lesbian reality dictated by a patriarchal and heterosexual world."[10]

By using the existing tropes and conventions, writing about women as sexually desirable objects, Peri Rossi, as a woman poet, calls into question both the universality of heterosexuality and the notion of the free-standing text. Meanings shift when the gender of the author is known. Even (or perhaps especially) when she uses a male persona, the effect of her erotic poem about a woman is the opposite of a man's. Whereas the man's poem reinscribes and reinforces traditional gender relations and traditional notions of sexuality, hers questions them. Whereas the man's poem upholds the idea that the poet/knower/speaker is male and that maleness is natural and unitary, with the easy coincidence of male poet and male speaker, the deployment of a male persona in Peri Rossi's poem unsettles and destabilizes received assumptions. If the maleness of the speaker does not devolve naturally from the maleness of the poet, gender can be taken on and cast off.

Peri Rossi's later, overtly lesbian poems, in which the speaker is a woman, sends us back to reread the earlier texts, if we were naive enough to believe that they weren't coded lesbian works all along. Attentive reading to those early poems shows that though the speaker is often male, the sexuality represented is not phallocentric and the sexual activity described or alluded to, though certainly within the heterosexual repertoire, is nothing that women cannot do without a man.[11] In other words, Peri Rossi's *Evohé* is lesbian poetry lightly coded, readable as heterosexual poetry because conventional erotic poetry has laid down tracks in our minds that would take us straight.

In her early work Peri Rossi often incorporates lesbian meanings in such a way that they can be disregarded by heterosexist readers, as in the reference to Sappho in the following discussion of the relation between politics and literature:

> La literatura es una forma de conocimiento, con sus características propias. . . . Y siempre depende en definitiva—muy, muy a la larga, a veces—del estado actual de la lucha de clases en un determinado país y en un momento histórico determinado. . . . Si partimos de la base de que cualquier producto artístico ordena la realidad según quien lo produce, ya en ese orden que es el artista al expresarse, implícitamente hay un mensaje, que no tiene porqué ser político. Sin embargo, si podemos entender por qué una manzana es política . . . habremos comprendido

por qué un cuento de Borges es político, o un poema de Safo lo es.
(Zeitz 83)

[Literature is a form of knowledge, with its own characteristics. . . . And
it always depends definitively—though in the very long run at times—on
the current state of the class struggle in a given country and a given
moment in history. . . . If we begin from the basic proposition that any
work of art orders reality according to who produces it, since in this
order it is the artist expressing himself, implicitly there is a message that
does not have to be political. Nevertheless, if we can understand how an
apple can be political . . . we will have understood why a story by
Borges is political, or why a poem by Sappho is.]

Insofar as bourgeois ideology reads lyric poetry as "nonpolitical,"
Sappho is to be understood as the quintessential apolitical poet, politicized only when everything, even fruit, is.[12] But Sappho is also the icon-
ographic lesbian poet, whose poetry is subversive in its celebration of
transgression. Peri Rossi does not resolve this ambiguity. In another instance, Peri Rossi's list of what literature can accommodate alongside its
"main" content is a series of terms suggesting otherness, what Lacanian
accounts define as the feminine, or difference. "Ambiguity, subterfuge,
evasion, confession, induction, seduction, incoherence, mysticism, eroticism, etc., etc." is how the list goes (see Zeitz 83). These elements, easily
understood with reference to transgressive sexuality, are presented as secondary, but they make such a long and compelling list that they suggest
that they are what her writing is, ultimately, all about.

At the same time, Peri Rossi claims that her literary commitment is to
knowledge, understood as a political phenomenon:

Mi compromiso es con el conocimiento, y a través de él, con el mundo y
mis semejantes. Mi obra intenta buscar, investigar, expresar, revelar, y
todo esto es política, aunque no haya el menor indicio de panfleto.
Ahora, la política entra en mi propia obra literaria por el mero hecho de
que soy víctima de la política desde el momento que nací. (Zeitz 83-84)

[My engagement is with knowledge, and through it, with the world and
my kind. My work tries to find, investigate, express, reveal, and all of
that is political, though there's not a trace of tendentiousness. Now then,
politics enters my own literary work by the mere fact that I have been a
victim of politics from the moment I was born.]

On this understanding, politics is both broadly defined and immediately experienced. What is political is everything that has to do with the
world, but also, specifically, it is about fascism in Uruguay. Sexuality is

clearly political in the former, less so in the second—until and unless you focus on the way fascism deals with lesbianism, which Peri Rossi does not.

In an interview with Susanna Ragazzoni Peri Rossi goes far in the direction of self-disclosure concerning the eroticism in her poetry, even saying that when she writes she has less sex. But she hedges around the issue of lesbianism:

> Para mí el erotismo y el escribir son dos cosas equivalentes; hasta te diría que la libido funciona tanto para hacer el amor como para escribir, hasta tal punto que me doy cuenta, en mi propia economía, que en los períodos en que escribo mucho tengo menos actividad sexual, porque se escribe con la misma parte. El estado con que escribo es un estado orgiástico. *Lo que quiero es escribir literatura erótica sin falsas máscaras. Asumir el rol homosexual cuando lo tengo que asumir, sin ningún tipo de disfraz*, no por provocación o exhibicionismo, sencillamente por amor a la libertad. La mía es una actividad más festiva, más orgiástica, que tiene un aspecto de deleite real. (241; emphasis added)

> [For me, eroticism and writing are two equivalent things; I'd even go so far as to say to you that the libido functions as much for lovemaking as for writing, to such an extent that I realize, in my own makeup, that in the periods in which I'm writing a great deal I have less sexual activity, because you write with the same part. The state I write in is an orgiastic state. *What I want is to write erotic literature without false masks. To assume the homosexual role when I have to assume it, without any sort of disguise*, not for the sake of provocation or exhibitionism, simply for the love of freedom. Mine is a more festive activity, more orgiastic, that has an aspect of real delight.][13]

Here Peri Rossi associates writing with bodiliness and sexuality, saying—ambiguously—that she wants to (not that she necessarily does) write homosexual poetry with no masks. But she also says she wants to *assume* the homosexual role, that is, take on the persona, which is precisely the masking she has just claimed to eschew.[14] Furthermore, the connection between bodiliness and writing at the beginning of this passage suggests not that she writes out of bodily experience but the contrary, that a kind of sublimation is going on, and that the eroticism of writing displaces the eroticism of sexual activity.

In the same interview Peri Rossi talks about *Evohé*:

> En *Evohé*, el esquema del libro es: la palabra y la mujer son dos símbolos iguales. Hay un juego permanente entre el poeta y el amante,

poeta-amante, mujer-palabra, son grupos de palabras equivalentes y
todo lo que se hace con las palabras se hace con la relación intelectual,
afectiva, con la mujer. Son símbolos con los cuales se tiene una relación
intelectual, afectiva, sensual, claro que cargo las tintas en la parte
sensual. De la misma manera que uno pesa un cuerpo, una palabra,
mide una palabra, mide un cuerpo. (241)

[In *Evohé*, the scheme of the book is that the word and the woman are
two coequal symbols. There is a permanent play between the poet and
the lover, poet-lover, word-woman; they are equivalent groups of words,
and everything that is done with the words is done with the intellectual,
affective relationship with the woman. The word and the woman are
symbols with which one has an intellectual, affective, sensual
relationship—of course I put more stress on the sensual part. In the
same way that one weighs a body, a word, one measures a word,
measures a body.]

Of course, one weighs and measures a body literally, and weighs and
measures words metaphorically. What is interesting here is the relation
between active and passive: poet is to word as lover is to woman, where
all the cultural baggage about who acts, and whom or what is acted
upon, remains unquestioned—except for the biographical fact that the
poet who is behind all this is herself a woman, speaking as subject. The
analogy is also belied by the book's first "real" poem (after the dedica-
tions, prologue, and epigraph, also poems of a sort), which marks the difference between women—troublesome creatures who come with their
own body, history, and claims on the speaker—and words, which are a
refuge from such demands:

> Cansado de mujeres,
> de historias terribles que ellas me contaban,
> cansado de la piel,
> de sus estremecimientos y solicitudes,
> como un ermitaño,
> me refugié en las palabras.

> [Weary of women,
> of terrible stories they would tell me,
> tired of my skin,
> of its trembling and importunings,

like a hermit,
I took refuge in words.][15]

Evohé rehearses the strain between woman *as* word (the two are in-
terchanged in several poems) and woman confined and masked *by* words.
Diáspora is largely concerned with deconstructing the masculine creation
of "woman" in language, particularly through poetry.[16] In the poems of
Diáspora women finally begin to resist their imprisonment in language.
The speakers in these poems are variously placed—as lover, jailer, detached observer, opinionated commentator—but they begin to share the
floor with the women, still caged or recently freed. The poet herself seems
to be negotiating a path between the two positions. In "Cacería para un
solo enamorado" (Hunting party for a lone lover) the speaker is the poet/
lover who painstakingly collects words and offers them to the beloved/
woman. The woman takes the carefully assembled words, received poetry
dedicated to her, casts them out the window, and speaks for herself, but
only to the man, who then reports her words: "¿Has visto?—me dijiste—
/ Al final no eran tan irresistibles" ("You see?" you said to me. / "In the
end they weren't so irresistible"). In the final poem of the collection, on
Lewis Carroll and Alice, the speaker identifies with the adult attracted to
little girls as well as with the little girl who steals the word to write her
own version of the story.[17]

The poem "Diáspora" is the centerpiece of the book, both because it
gives the collection its title and because it is positioned midway between
beginning and end of the volume. It is also the longest piece and one of
the few that has any narrative content. A poem about desire, loss, anger,
disdain, about being excluded and not belonging anyway, it takes up the
condition of the exile. The speaker is not identifiable as either male or
female, but the reading of the poem changes significantly by assuming the
speaker is of one gender or the other. The speaker addresses a desired
woman who eludes him/her and finally earns his/her disdain. The speaker
is, to a certain extent, sympathetic. S/he alludes to the military takeover
that resulted in her/his situation, and the point of view is of the excluded
speaker, whose longing and anger are both perfectly understandable. But
his/her attitude toward the desired woman is problematic, especially
when he/she accuses her of being sunk in vice. The woman's wicked hab-
its include promiscuity and smoking hashish, and if the speaker is a man
she is "accused" of miscegenation and lesbianism as vices. If it is a

woman, the line "I know you like women" is a sign of hope and possible connection, a positive sign—quite the opposite of what it means if a man is speaking. If the speaker is a man, he is more readily separated from the poet, and the racism and homophobia can be assumed to be his and not hers. On the other hand, to assume a woman speaker, a lesbian and an exile from Latin America, is to draw a much closer association between speaker and poet, a problematic association since it suggests that the intelligence drawing the poem is in agreement with both the appropriateness of the desired woman's fondness for women and the speaker's racism. Since the poem is deliberately evasive on the matter of the gender of the speaker (it takes some doing to avoid all those gender-inflected pronouns and adjectives), the reader is caught between a conventional, culturally determined heterosexist reading and a lesbian reading prompted by the also conventional association between speaker and poet that cannot be resolved.

Peri Rossi's prose in the post-Uruguayan period—*Una pasión prohibida* (A forbidden passion), *La nave de los locos* (Ship of Fools), *Solitario de amor* (Loner/Lover), *Cosmoagonías* (Cosmoagonies), as well as the books discussed in chapter 3—deals with lesbianism peripherally, if at all.[18] Nor is lesbianism, even when clearly represented as such, always presented as politically progressive. Several of Peri Rossi's early texts do deal with the eroticized power differential in lesbian relationships, however. In the first story of *Viviendo* (1963), a sexually repressed middle-class woman hires a maid who must share her bedroom, and a later story concerns a sexually obsessed queen whose favorite pastime is the sexual exploitation of her slaves. A series of poems in *Diáspora* (1976) have as their central figure the bacchante, a bored and dissolute bourgeoise who desires her heterosexually identified maid, and the poems in which the speaker is distracted by the charms of little girls suggest the sexual attraction inherent in power differentials. A particularly haunting and disturbing poem in *Descripción de un naufragio* (1975) has a sexually ambiguous speaker (ostensibly a man given the generic masculine of the rest of the book), sexual activity that could be lesbian, and a "beloved" so passive as to seem dead. None of these stories/poems links lesbianism to freedom; they tend toward a representation of an obsessive sexuality whose function is to mask some inner terror or lack. In other poems, lesbianism is healing, joyful, but intimate in that it is directed inward, between the lovers, rather than outward toward a vindication of rights or a transformational politics.

In *Lingüística general* (1979), Peri Rossi begins with a series of poems on language and meaning. She adds the question of gender with a poem that seems to use a random word as exemplar of linguistic problem. But that word is "she," and the investigation of it is of course not random at all:

> *Ella* es ella más todas las veces que leí
> la palabra *ella* escrita en cualquier texto
> más las veces que soñé *ella*
> más sus evocaciones,
> diferentes a las mías. (emphasis in the original)

> [*She* is she plus all the times I read
> the word *she* written in any text
> plus the times I dreamt *she*
> plus its evocations,
> different than mine.]

The meaning of "she" accumulates in the empty spaces left by heterosexist discourse, and accrues to the already-existing meanings of the word generated by that discourse. This desire to redefine not just "woman," but the abstract grammatical term, the pronoun, that signals her displacement, culminates in another kind of difference—not gender difference, between "he" and "she" (for "he" is immaterial in this poem), but lesbian difference, internal to the marker "woman".[19] Since the gender of the speaker remains unmarked, my reading of the poem relies on the assumptions I bring to it.

The speaker of the early poems in *Lingüística general* is not clearly gendered, and the themes of love and desire that run through the collection heighten the ambiguity. Familiarity with Peri Rossi's earlier poetry, in which the voice is almost always either male or unmarked, together with her purportedly conventional use of the generic masculine, supports a male-voiced reading. But the ambiguity is broken toward the end of the collection with a coming-out poem that revises the previous poems:

> Esta noche, entre todos los normales,
> te invito a cruzar el puente.
> Nos mirarán con curiosidad—*estas dos muchachas*—
> y quizás, si somos lo suficientemente sabias,

secretas y sutiles
perdonen nuestra subversión
sin necesidad de llamar al médico
el comisario político o al cura.

[Tonight, among all the normal people
I invite you to cross the bridge.
They will look at us with curiosity—*these two girls*—
and perhaps if we are sufficiently wise,
discreet and subtle
they will forgive our subversion
without having to call the doctor
the political commissar or the priest.]

The poem expresses a barely contained passion, desire as yet unfulfilled:

Y el vaporetto se desliza suavemente
entre estas flores blancas sin tocarlas
rozándolas apenas
como ronda el deseo en pos de ti
en pos de mí
densa película que nos unta
enardeciente,
húmeda,
cual y semejante.

[And the vaporetto glides softly
among these white flowers, not touching them
barely grazing them
like desire at your heels,
at mine,
dense oily film covering us
impassioned,
damp,
so
alike.]

The poem contains the reasons for the speaker's reluctance to come all the way out of the closet—the weight of science, politics, and religion is likely to come crashing down on the lovers if they are too openly transgressive. By the next poem, though, the tone is no longer that of tentative desire, but celebration and joy in flouting convention as part of the pleasure of their lovemaking. That is, the pleasure of refusing to hide, refusing heterosexuality, refusing to fetishize difference, of openly subverting the "domestic order." In this last poem of the book, the lovers thumb their noses at naturalized difference.

> Te amo esta y otras noches
> con las señas de identidad
> cambiadas
> como alegremente cambiamos nuestras ropas
> y tu vestido es el mío
> y mis sandalias son las tuyas
> Como mi seno
> es tu seno
> y tus antepasadas son las mías . . .
> y a la noche quizás salgamos a pasear
> tú o yo vestida de varón
> y la otra de mujer
> como consagra
> el uso de la especie
> y consejo divino:
> Creced y dividíos
> Multiplicaos en vano.
>
> [I love you this and other nights
> with our signs of identity
> exchanged
> as joyfully as we switch clothes
> and your dress is mine
> and my sandals are yours
> As my breast
> is your breast

and your ancient mothers are my own . . .
and at night we might go out for a walk
you or I dressed as a man
and the other as a woman
as the custom of the species
and holy advice
decree:
Be fruitful and divide
Multiply in vain.]

   This offhand defiance of the laws of god and man consists of assuming
one or the other gender provisionally, and by choice. Butch and femme
are not preordained by some im/balance of hormones but by whim and
fancy; they are a matter of performance. Furthermore, the sexual pleasure of differentiation/division is severed from reproduction, which is its
opposite: multiplication. When self-generated, differentiation is a source
of pleasure and creativity, and not the reinscription of a pointless, merely
procreation-driven gender division.
   Here travesty, taking on male dress (or the male voice), enhances
textual/sexual pleasure. At this juncture, though, travesty is no longer a
safety device, as in the early poems when Peri Rossi the poet could retreat
into the male voice to cover up the lesbian text. Butch and femme do not
imitate heterosexual behavior so much as parody it. The elements of
transgression and of the easy reversibility of who is the man and who is
the woman contradict and undermine the supposition of inevitable heterosexuality based on immutable sex, undifferentiated from gender.
   What makes the encoding of lesbianism finally unnecessary in Peri
Rossi's poetry is a combination of poetic maturity, the fact of exile, and a
separation between her lesbian and nonlesbian writing. Peri Rossi's earliest writing consists of stories pervaded by a submerged lesbianism. The
stories of *Viviendo* are traditional, in the sense that they develop characters, use dialogue and description, evoke place and time, have plots, and
often even provide a twist at the end. Unlike most of her later fiction they
are protagonized by women, who are all more or less unaware of their
own sexual attraction to other women, and these early stories read as
much like tales of sadly unsuccessful heterosexuality as they do of sadly
thwarted lesbianism. Such subsequent collections of Peri Rossi's short
narrative as *Los museos abandonados* (The abandoned museums, 1968),

Indicios pánicos (Panic signs, 1970), *El museo de los esfuerzos inútiles* (The museum of futile efforts, 1983), *Una pasión prohibida*, and *Cosmoagonías* are more modernist in their minimization of plot and character. Expressive rather than narrative, they are more like essays or poems. The relationship between politics and consciousness assumes greater and greater urgency in them, as the political situation in Uruguay goes from precarious to disastrous. Sexuality takes on a secondary role—the fixed element in the metaphor, if evoked at all. Transgressive sexuality (incest, children's sexual activity) is related to impending political catastrophe. The apparently male-identified poems of *Evohé* are also from this period, and, like the stories of *Viviendo*, they do not deal with overtly political questions. When disaster strikes, in the form of the military coup, sexuality becomes unconditionally relegated to the back burner. *Descripción de un naufragio* not only fails to deal with exploration in lesbian sexuality, it in fact relies on heterosexual and misogynistic traditional constructions of women's sexuality in formulating its denunciation of the military dictatorship that resulted in so much torture, disappearance, death, and exile. When Peri Rossi comes back to lesbianism in *Lingüística general,* it is to celebrate an openly lesbian relationship, in which part of the pleasure of the lovers is flaunting their transgressive relationship. On the one hand, there is a recognition that their sexual liberation is in fact part of the revolution, but on the other, the lesbian poems are parenthetical. They are about lovers on vacation, not only in exile but on a train trip out of the new country. The section is set off from the rest of the book, and it is joyful and playful—not the tone that Peri Rossi is best known for. In fact the literary respect she has garnered has to do with the impersonality and severity of her prose writing, where any play takes the form of grim irony.

As an exile on holiday, the speaker takes advantage of the freedom of just passing through to make coming out feasible, but the holiday is also a journey of return. Italy is the ancestral homeland that Peri Rossi never inhabited, but which is the place of her own ancient mothers as well as those the lovers share in her poem of celebration. Crossing the bridge to a textually open lesbianism becomes a kind of return to a deeper self.

Yet taken together, Peri Rossi's representations of lesbianism suggest that her work is not the simple map of a unitary consciousness. Ultimately, she calls into question the relationship between the poet and the speaker in such a way that it is possible neither to separate them categorically nor unite them categorically, but rather to engage in prismatic readings of the poems, in which the reader embraces the poems' ambiguity, reading the speaker now as a woman, now as a man, now as one with Peri Rossi, now not. Other poems address a "you" that might or might not be a trope for the self. The refusal to accept gender as an absolute enables these multiple readings, and gender ceases to be an absolute in part because the absolute division into gender as a function of the naturalness of heterosexuality is contested in the work. Once lesbianism is a possibility, once the conventions of heterosexual and heterosexist love poetry are challenged by their very repetition in the mouth of a person of the "wrong" sex, the whole structure of gender differentiation and hierarchy, as well as the notion of the single right reading of the poem, is called into question. Ambiguity reigns in the poetry as a beacon, an idealistic solution for the rigidity of heterosexism that manifests itself through the ferocity of homophobia, and for the single-mindedness of an authoritarian government that terrorizes where it cannot impose control. In her most joyful lesbian poem Peri Rossi enjoins her reader to "be fruitful and divide," recalling the promise of mitotic unfolding for the women in exile of chapter 3.

Peri Rossi's deliberate ambiguity is countered in a very few poems that construe transgressive, and particularly lesbian, sexuality as integral to a revolutionary agenda. In a short, ostensibly simple poem in *Diáspora,* the speaker addresses the [male] poets who have undressed "woman" time and time again in their texts, reducing her to their specifications. The woman Peri Rossi opposes to this blow-up doll is a lesbian with her own sexual and political agenda. She is a specific, individual woman, located in a particular time and place; and she is, simultaneously, coded universal. Located in New York, her placard/text is in English and French, two foreign languages embedded in this Spanish poem. She is self-defining, "Je suis lesbianne," and self-evaluating, "I am beautiful." Her beauty is not conferred on her by the male gaze or androcentric discourse, but claimed—and not for men, but for herself and for other women. Her self-sufficient splendor is offered up as a challenge by a new poetic voice, the lesbian poet who now possesses the gaze in order to admire this woman who even as object is subject.[20]

A los poetas que alabaron su desnudez
les diré:
mucho mejor que ella quitándose el vestido
es ella desfilándose por las calles de Nueva York

—Park Avenue—
con un cartel que dice:
"Je suis lesbianne. I am beautiful."

[To the poets who praised her nakedness
I shall say:
much better than she, taking off her dress,
is she, marching through the streets of New York
—Park Avenue—
with a sign that says:
"Je suis lesbianne. *I am beautiful.*"]

In the international, cosmopolitan context, lesbianism as a political position, in opposition to sexist and heterosexist oppression, becomes possible. After Peri Rossi is exiled from Uruguay, the ambiguous lesbianism of her works separates itself out and becomes, if less frequent, more direct.

Afterword
In the Realm of the Real

Latin American feminist criticism, however academic, is a return to the concrete. It is a criticism that, through both its sources, understands the power and treachery of language, a language that belongs to the other—the privileged male subject or the powerful apparatus of the state, or the mass media, or the European colonizer—a language, therefore, that must be stolen, asserted, reinvented, always treated cautiously. Where so much is at stake, the mesmerizing effects of pure theory are brought up short with a jolt, and history, ethics, and responsibility are brought forcefully back into play.

This book, then, has been about writing and reading as material acts in the world. It is about agency and the possibility of transformation. It is for two groups of readers who do not usually talk together, but whose conversations resonate with each other's, whose practices each have something vital to offer each other. This book is, in the broadest sense, about the feminist demetaphorization of the language of sexuality for Latin Americanists and the Latin Americanist derhetorization of the language of politics for feminists.

At the beginning of chapter 2 I cited three authors who use sexuality as metaphor for some aspect of nation-making. One of them, however, disrupts the calm surface of reified sexuality that makes such rhetorical use possible. An unnamed couple in Marta Lynch's crowd reanimates sex for its own sake. For them, stimulated by the excitement of the political rally, sex is sex, with its own meaning, and its own pleasure. Both sex and politics are going on, at the same time, neither subordinated to the other, but rather in a reciprocal relationship. This reciprocity is what I have tried to articulate in the previous chapters, sometimes focusing on one issue more sharply than another, but never, I hope, losing sight of their connection.

Neither nation-making nor sexuality is the be-all and end-all of Latin American women's writing. Not every tale is a story of gendered sex, not all stories are national allegories. Reading for the complexity of meanings of sexuality, gender, and politics is, nevertheless, a necessary starting point if we are to disturb the impassive solidity of prepackaged truths and uninterrogated assumptions that have thus far prevented us from seeing our way into a new history.

Notes

Introduction

1. See, for example, Sara Castro-Klarén, "La crítica literaria feminista y la escritora en América Latina," *La sartén por el mango: Encuentro de escritoras latinoamericanas,* Patricia Elena González and Eliana Ortega, eds. (Río Piedras, Puerto Rico: Ediciones Huracán, 1984); 27-46; and Gabriela Mora, "Un diálogo entre feministas hispanoamericanas," *Cultural and Historical Grounding for Hispanic and Luso-Brazilian Feminist Literary Criticism,* Hernán Vidal, ed. (Minneapolis: Institute for the Study of Ideologies and Literature, 1989), 53-78.

2. See, for example, Diane Marting, *Fifty Spanish American Women Writers* (Westport, Conn.: Greenwood Press, 1989); Beth Miller, ed., *Women in Hispanic Literature: Icons and Fallen Idols* (Berkeley: University of California Press, 1983); Patricia Elena González and Eliana Ortega, eds., *La sartén por el mango: Encuentro de escritoras latinoamericanas.*

3. Evelyn Picon Garfield, *Women's Voices from Latin America: Interviews with Six Contemporary Authors* (Detroit: Wayne State University, 1985) and Magdalena García Pinto, *Historias íntimas: Conversaciones con diez escritoras latinoamericanas* (Hanover, N.H.: Ediciones del Norte, 1988). The Chilean poet Marjorie Agosin has assembled several volumes of Latin American women's writing in translation. One of many recent collections is *Beyond the Border: A New Age in Latin American Women's Fiction,* Nora Erro-Peralta and Caridad Silva-Nuñez, eds. (San Francisco: Cleis Press, 1991).

4. See, especially, Jean Franco, *Plotting Women* (New York: Columbia University Press, 1989); the Seminar on Feminism and Culture in Latin America's *Women, Culture and Politics in Latin America* (Berkeley: University of California Press, 1989); and Doris Sommer, *Foundational Fictions* (Princeton: Princeton University Press, 1990).

5. Roberto González Echevarría, "The Criticism of Latin American Literature Today: Adorno, Molloy, Magnarelli," *Profession* 87 (1987): 10-13. The other two critics González

Echevarría praises are also women, Rolena Adorno and Sylvia Molloy. The fact that the literary texts he recalls are all written by men and the criticism is all by women suggests that González Echevarría is aware on some level of the gender issues he does not address directly in his piece.

6. Given the potential of overtly feminist work to scandalize and alienate its readers, the subversive possibilities of feminist scholarship that does not announce itself as such should not be underestimated. Doris Sommer's *Foundational Fictions* is a case in point. Like Magnarelli in *The Lost Rib* (Lewisburg: Bucknell University Press, 1985), Sommer deals primarily with male authors of canonical texts. It is also worth noting that Magnarelli's study of Luisa Valenzuela's fiction, *Reflections/Refractions: Reading Luisa Valenzuela* (New York: Peter Lang, 1988) has received neither the acclaim nor the audience *The Lost Rib* has, though it is an equally fine piece of scholarship.

7. Eliana Rivero, "Otra vez la(s) palabra(s) terrible(s): precisiones de lo femenino y lo feminista en la práctica literaria hispanoamericana," unpublished paper presented at the conference "Feminism, Writing, and Politics in Hispanic and Luso-Brazilian Culture and Literature" (University of Minnesota, October 1990) makes a similar point in her discussion of feminist neocolonialism, arguing that the corrective and necessary focus on difference among women should not erase the similarities among women's situations across class and culture that make feminism possible as a coherent political movement.

8. See Catherine MacKinnon, "Feminism, Marxism, Method and the State: An Agenda for Theory," *Signs: A Journal of Women in Culture and Society* 7, no. 3 (spring 1982): 515-44; Gayle Rubin, "The Traffic in Women: Notes on the 'Political Economy' of Sex," *Toward an Anthropology of Women*, Reyna Rapp Reiter, ed. (New York: Monthly Review Press, 1975), and Adrienne Rich "Compulsory Heterosexuality and Lesbian Existence," *Signs: A Journal of Women in Culture and Society* 5, no. 4 (summer 1980): 631-60, for early and influential discussions of women's sexual subordination and of the link between it and what Rich calls "compulsory heterosexuality."

9. Any critique of homophobia and heterosexism to take hold in Latin America will undoubtedly attach itself to the left, just as traditional sexist attitudes and behavior that cross the political spectrum have become less respectable on the left with the rise of international feminism. Perhaps the best-known novelistic treatment of the relationship between politics and sexuality is Manuel Puig's *El beso de la mujer araña*, in which the revolutionary "hero" must question his sexism, his homophobia, and his class assumptions when he is confronted with his ostensibly apolitical homosexual cellmate.

10. Ana Vásquez, "Feminismo: Dudas y contradicciones," *Nueva Sociedad* 78 (July-August 1985, special issue, "Las mujeres: la mayoría marginada"): 55-61, notes the homophobia among Latin American feminists themselves. Though she deplores the internal discrimination against lesbians, she does not consider the importance of specifically lesbian contributions to the feminist movement.

11. The IV Encuentro Feminista Latinoamericano y del Caribe, reported on in the Peruvian feminist magazine *Viva* 13 (March 1988): 19-27 (especially p. 22), included a lesbian workshop that generated the following goals: to gain space within the feminist movement, to build a lesbian identity, and to reject discrimination. The publications from earlier Encuentros have also included reports from lesbian workshops, which, unlike other reports, were submitted without naming the workshop leaders.

12. It is not surprising that Franco has emerged as a feminist critic. Though not a pioneer in the field, Franco's work in this area lends credibility and prestige to Latin American feminist criticism, not simply because it is in itself meritorious (which it most indisputably is), but because Franco has done outstanding nonfeminist work in the past, for which she has earned the respect of the critical establishment.

13. Most Americans agree with them. Reading novels is considered an appropriate pastime for receptionists and housewives—two of the most disrespected groups of women in this culture—and poetry is associated with dreamy-eyed young women at expensive liberal arts colleges, who are still primarily construed as decorative prizes. The cultural discourse functions to devalue both women and literature in a mutually reinforcing manner. Recent right-wing attacks on artists and writers, however, suggest that this derision functions to mask fear.

1. Translating Gender

1. Spanish is widely considered the easiest foreign language to learn, and not because almost all the letters in almost all the words are pronounced. When the majority Anglo culture complacently considers a minority as not very bright, how can its language be difficult, or complicated, or subtle?

2. At the 1988 conference on feminist criticism and Iberian and Latin American literatures held at the University of Minnesota, in which the common language was Spanish, a long discussion was generated by one participant's expression of her discomfort with the term *género*. This single lexical item thus became a major point of the agenda for the last day's session devoted to a consideration of the conference as a whole. Though much of the discussion was practical, consisting of suggestions about how to fill the perceived lexical gap, the energy devoted to the topic implied that the issue concerned more than a question of a recalcitrant noun.

3. In "The Technology of Gender," chapter 1 of *Technologies of Gender: Essays on Theory, Film, and Fiction* (Bloomington: Indiana University Press, 1987), de Lauretis discusses briefly the lack of distinction between sex and gender in Romance languages: "The second meaning of *gender* given in the dictionary is 'classification of sex; sex.' This proximity of grammar and sex, interestingly enough, is not there in Romance languages (which, it is commonly believed, are spoken by people rather more romantic than Anglo-Saxons). The Spanish *género*, the Italian *genere,* and the French *genre* do not carry even the connotation of a person's gender; that is conveyed by the word for sex. And for this reason, it would seem, the word *genre,* adopted from the French to refer to the specific classification of artistic and literary forms (in the first place, painting), is also devoid of any sexual denotation, as is the word *genus,* the Latin etymology of gender, used in English as a classificatory word in biology and logic. An interesting corollary of this linguistic peculiarity of English, i.e., the acceptation of gender which refers to sex, is that the notion of gender I am discussing, and thus the whole tangled question of the relationship of human gender to representation, are totally untranslatable in any Romance language, a sobering thought for anyone who might still be tempted to espouse an internationalist, not to say universal, view of the project of theorizing gender" (4).

4. See, for example, Donna Haraway, *Primate Visions: Gender, Race, and Nature in the World of Modern Science* (New York: Routledge, 1989), especially page 342.

5. Discussions with members of the Forum for Women's Studies (Kvinnoforsknings-seminariet), University of Umeå, Umeå, Sweden, 1984. More recently some Swedish academics have taken up the heretofore solely grammatical term, *genus.*

6. Though the growth of feminism in Latin America has been slowed by the abuse it has suffered from both the right and the left, it is important to note its existence as a political movement, if much less as an academic or theoretical process. Women's oppression as women is beginning to be recognized on the left, even among men, as a legitimate claim.

7. Many feminist critics writing in English have played on the gender/genre near pun. None has demonstrated a convincing correlation between the two.

8. See chapter 2 for a further discussion of this song.

9. Luisa Valenzuela, "Five Days That Changed My Paper," presentation at the annual convention of the Modern Language Association of America, Chicago, December 1990. Valenzuela's talk was exciting for a number of reasons, not least of which was that she gave large parts of it in Spanish, thus claiming for Spanish the status of a language important for scholars to understand.

10. Eliana Rivero, in "Otra vez la(s) palabra(s) terrible(s)," points out that Carmen Conde, who applied the term *poetisa* to herself and to the women poets she anthologized, singled out Gabriela Mistral as "un gran poeta mujer," using the masculine as a form of praise and appending the noun (*mujer* = woman) rather than the adjective (*femenino* = feminine/woman) to clarify her gender.

11. Reassessing essentialism is a risky business when (1) the aim of feminism is to free women from oppression on the grounds of bodily difference, and (2) "essentialism" is an epithet to hurl, and those who claim that differences between men and women are immutable are presumed to be naive. Nevertheless, the quasi-automatic response to the epithet "essentialist" is now being assessed by feminist theorists.

12. See, for example, Denise Riley, *"Am I That Name?": Feminism and the Category of "Women" in History* (Minneapolis: University of Minnesota Press, 1988).

13. Carmen Naranjo, *La Mujer y el desarrollo. La mujer y la cultura: antología* (Mexico City: UNICEF/Diana, 1981), 1.

14. Grammatically, the "neutral" form of the adjective is identical to the masculine singular, and its neuter form, *lo feminino* ("that which is feminine"), also appears suspiciously masculine. The apparent internal contradiction between semantics and morphology is particularly striking to the nonnative speaker.

15. Julieta Kirkwood, "Feministas y políticas," *Nueva Sociedad* 78 (July-August 1985, special issue, "Las mujeres: la mayoría marginada"): 62-70, particularly page 64. All translations from this article are my own.

16. Julieta Kirkwood, "El feminismo como negación del autoritarismo," paper presented to the feminist studies group, Clacso, Buenos Aires, December 4, 1983 (see *Material de discusión programa FLACSO-Santiago de Chile*, no. 52, December 1983, 143-155). All translations from this article are my own. In this article Kirkwood points out the need to discuss the articulation of class and gender, a necessity that middle-class North American feminists were just beginning to discover: "Retomando aspectos más generales, diríamos que para las concepciones ortodoxas de izquierda o derecha, el tema que se plantea no es, ni ha sido, el problema de la búsqueda de 'significados' a lo que positivamente podría ser o es—y cómo es—'hacer política' desde las mujeres, considerando el lugar que ocupan dentro de la sociedad, vale decir, articulando clase y género" (151) ["Going back to more general aspects, we would say that for the orthodox conceptions of right or left, the theme that is proposed is not, and has not been, the problem of the search for 'signifieds' to determine positively what it could be or is—and how it is—to 'make politics' starting from women, considering the place they occupy in society, that it is to say, articulating class and gender"].

17. Ana Vásquez, "Feminismo: Dudas y contradicciones." All translations from this article are my own.

18. From the earliest stages of North American feminism, the issue of naming one's own experience, of wresting the language from patriarchal control, deconstructing the dominant discourse, special attention paid to how, by whom, and to whose benefit women had been named, led to a continued vigilance concerning language. Words are chosen carefully, since language is booby-trapped. Even in words that do not apparently carry gender meanings, gender is often hidden: the shift from mailman to letter carrier, together with the increasing number of women who deliver the post, may work to some extent in changing the

mental image of the person doing that task, but "CEO" still signifies male, even though nothing in the term explicitly designates it as such. Language also remains a site of conflict within Latin America, where censorship (both official, such as governments ordering books off shelves, and unofficial, like death squads killing writers) is a pervasive threat, and where there is a history of repressive governments controlling the mass media and representing activity and individuals to their own benefit. Repression is called democracy in Christiani's El Salvador; student protesters were communist revolutionaries in Pinochet's Chile; the Mothers of the Plaza de Mayo were the madwomen of Videla's Argentina. The levels of cynicism in languages of representation must not be ignored.

19. Patricia Pinto Villarroel, "Mirada y voz femeninas en la ensayística de Amanda Labarca: Historia de una anticipación chilena," *Nuevo Texto Crítico* 2, no. 4 (1989, special issue, *América Latina: Mujer, Escritura, Praxis*): 57-68.

2. Gender as Category and Feminism as Strategy in Latin American Literary Analysis

1. Both excerpts are from *Canto general*, taken from *Neruda and Vallejo: Selected Poems*, Robert Bly, ed. (Boston: Beacon Press, 1971), 96-99 and 84-87. I depart from Bly's translation in the first excerpt, from "Himno y regreso," particularly in maintaining the gender of the child.

2. Octavio Paz, "Los hijos de la Malinche," *El laberinto de la soledad* (*Cuadernos Americanos,* 1950; reprint, Mexico City: Fondo de Cultura Económica, 1959), 72, 77; my translation.

3. Marta Lynch, *La alfombra roja* (Buenos Aires: Losada, 1966, repr. 1968), 10-11; my translation.

4. Recent work in anthropology and sociology have paid attention to function of gender in the social construction of reality. See, for example, Lourdes Benería and Martha Roldán, *The Crossroads of Class and Gender: Industrial Homework, Subcontracting, and Household Dynamics in Mexico City* (Chicago: University of Chicago Press, 1987).

5. See, for example, Marcelo Coddou on Chilean women's poetry and Pinochet's use of gender ideology in "La poesía femenina chilena como contratexto," *Signos* (Chile) 1, no. 3 (1984): 42-44.

6. See, for example, Juliet Mitchell, *Feminism and Psychoanalysis* (New York: Pantheon, 1974); Dorothy Dinnerstein, *The Mermaid and the Minotaur: Sexual Arrangements and the Human Malaise* (New York: Harper and Row, 1976); and Nancy Chodorow, *The Reproduction of Mothering: Psychoanalysis and the Sociology of Gender* (Berkeley: University of California Press, 1978). For a more recent discussion, see Jane Flax, *Thinking Fragments: Psychoanalysis, Feminism, and Postmodernism in the Contemporary West* (Berkeley: University of California Press, 1990), especially chapter 5.

7. Similarly, Rey Chow, *Woman and Chinese Modernity* (Minneapolis: University of Minnesota Press, 1990) discusses the currently untenable position of the "ethnic reader," women from colonized places with Western education.

8. It is important to acknowledge the middle-class roots of at least one part of the feminist movement that, beginning in the nineteenth century, took as its goals women's suffrage and access to higher education, both of which were of primary interest to women whose basic economic needs were already taken care of. Progressive women in Latin America have been divided into two camps: *políticas,* whose primary allegiance is to leftist political movements, and *feministas,* who have concentrated on gender-specific issues. In the past few years (thanks, in great extent, to the Encuentros Feministas), these groups have begun a di-

alogue, which, although not always friendly, has helped both sides question their own limitations and develop the scope of their theory and practice.

9. Under the leadership of Jean Franco, the Latin American Studies Association's 1991 convention featured a series of panels on women's issues in which progressive women activists—both *políticas* and *feministas*—participated, creating a space in Latin American academic discourse for their issues. Within Latin America it is important to recognize the distinction between social science and the humanities, which I perhaps too easily elide here. In some universities, the social sciences (particularly anthropology and sociology) have been more receptive to politically engaged scholarship than the humanities have.

10. This familiar phenomenon is often unacknowledged in such status quo modes of analysis as New Criticism, which prescribe that the text should be unconnected to social and political issues.

11. This is not to suggest that the political parties do not or should not have their feminist wings.

12. Katrina Irving, "(Still) Hesitating on the Threshold: Feminist Theory and the Question of the Subject," *NWSA Journal* 1, no. 4 (summer 1989): 630-43, maintains that any prediscursive reading of "experience" is wrongheaded, that the subject is only constructed in and through discourse. Interestingly she does this by looking at the use of the terms "home" and "exile"—and without ever paying attention to the literal meaning of exile, the one that determines the Latin American experience. She ultimately opts for a notion of identity as temporary stabilization.

13. I insist on using the term "consciousness-raising" as the perfectly good English translation of the Spanish *concientización*. The ugly neologism "concientization" functions only to erase the fact that in the United States this process derives from the women's movement, which in turn borrowed the practice from revolutionary China and, more to the point here, Cuba.

14. Patricia J. Williams, an African American feminist legal scholar, writes in *The Alchemy of Race and Rights* (Cambridge: Harvard University Press, 1991): "My parents were always telling me to look up at the world; to look straight at people, particularly white people; not to let them stare me down; to hold my ground; *to insist on the right to my presence no matter what*" (22, emphasis added).

15. Sylvia Molloy's discussion of Victoria Ocampo takes advantage of this aspect of presence: "I read [Ocampo's] references to her body in the autobiography as signifying something more complex—something that surely includes the concretely physical but goes beyond it, something more like a *presence* (the way one speaks of a presence on stage) that society would have her repress and for which her body is the most visible sign" [*At Face Value: Autobiographical Writing in Spanish America* (Cambridge: Cambridge University Press, 1991), 70, emphasis in the original].

16. The relationship between Chicano and Latin American phenomena is complex. Language and history are both partially shared, but the position of Chicanas between two cultures has too often been responsible for their invisibility in both. See Gloria Anzaldúa, *Borderlands/La frontera: La nueva mestiza* (San Francisco: Sisters/Aunt Lute, 1987).

3. The Presence in Absence of Exile

1. "Let everyone know, once and for all: / Exile cannot be just rhetoric anymore," from "Estado de exilio," *Las voces distantes: Antología de los creadores uruguayos de la diáspora*, Alvaro Barros-Lémez, ed. (Montevideo: Monte Sexto, 1985), 257. Portions of this chapter appeared in earlier forms as "Kvinner i eksil: Tre latinamerikansk forfattare," *Oppbrudd: Skrivende kvinner over hele verden*, Anne-Cathrine Andersen, Gerd Bjørhovde,

and Åse Hiorth Lervik, eds. (Tromsø/Oslo/Bergen/Stavanger: Universitetsförlaget, 1985), 225-35, and "Gender and Exile in Cristina Peri Rossi," *Selected Proceedings of the Wichita State University Conference on Foreign Literature*, Eunice Myers and Ginette Adamson, eds. (Lanham, Md.: University Press of America, 1987), 149-59.

2. See, for example, Luce Irigaray, *This Sex Which Is Not One* (Ithaca: Cornell University Press, 1985) and Julia Kristeva's observation that there is no such thing as (a) woman, "Women's Time," *Signs: A Journal of Women in Culture and Society* 7, no. 1 (autumn 1981):13-35. The effort of some women writers to assert a nongendered presence within this system, such as Marta Traba's "Hipótesis sobre una escritura diferente," *fem* 6, no. 22 (February-March 1982): 9-12 postulating a "different writing," for example, is doomed to fail, since presence itself is assumed to be masculine.

3. Though it is by far shorter than the typical *crónica,* Isabel de Guevara's text is like those of other chroniclers in its self-interest. She describes her own heroism and that of other women in the struggle to claim territory, so that she might be appropriately rewarded for her troubles.

4. Electa Arenal and Stacey Schlau have begun to address this lacuna with the publication of *Untold Sisters: Hispanic Nuns in Their Own Work* (Albuquerque: University of New Mexico Press, 1989).

5. The "Boom" is the name given to Latin America's entrance onto the scene of international literature in the late 1960s. It is most often associated with such names as Gabriel García Márquez, Mario Vargas Llosa, Carlos Fuentes, and Julio Cortázar.

6. Angel Rama, "Los contestarios del poder," *Novísimos narradores hispanoamericanos en marcha, 1964-1980,* Angel Rama, ed. (Mexico City: Marcha Editores, 1981), 17 (my translation).

7. Jane Marcus, "Alibis and Legends: The Ethics of Elsewhereness, Gender, and Estrangement," *Women's Writing in Exile,* Mary Lynn Broe and Angela Ingram, eds. (Chapel Hill: University of North Carolina Press, 1989), 269-94, rightly contends that the place of exile is not simply "elsewhere," but also somewhere. But Saúl Sosnowski, "Las otras fronteras: Literatura argentina en el exilio," *Discurso Literario* 2, no. 1: 233-42, points out that it can take a very long time for an exile to connect with that "somewhere else." In what may turn out to be Luisa Valenzuela's last exile text, written after many years' residence in the United States, the place of exile, the New York of *Novela negra con argentinos* (Hanover, N.H.: Ediciones del Norte, 1990; English title: Black novel with Argentines), is fully inhabited. Its two protagonists are unmistakably and irredeemably Argentinian despite their intimate knowledge of the place and their obsessive masking and unmasking of identity, decorating and permuting clothing, hair, beard, eyeglasses. The novel is about coming to terms with the ostensibly New York act of random violence, in this instance committed by an Argentinian. The echo chamber connection between the sexual violence of the United States and the political violence of Argentina is never fully resolved or even made definitive; the exile's sense of suspension and of discomforting difference does not go away.

8. "Censorship and the Female Writer—An Interview/Dialogue with Luisa Valenzuela," in Sharon Magnarelli, *Reflections/Refractions,* 211-12. This interview took place in 1981, before democracy was returned to Argentina.

9. Gabriela Mistral (1889-1957), born in Montegrande in north central Chile, became known as a poet in 1914, when she won a national poetry contest for her "Sonetos de la muerte" (Sonnets of death). Besides being a teacher and poet, she was also a diplomat, for which reason she spent much of her adult life outside Chile. Between 1922 and 1928 she resided in different parts of France, Spain, and Italy. Later, she lived in Brazil and finally in the United States, where she died. Her poems were fairly widely translated, and in 1945 Mistral became the first Latin American to win the Nobel Prize for literature. The Chilean

government had considered Mistral something of a natural resource even before 1945; winning the Nobel merely consolidated her privileged position. The official version of Mistral is that she was an asexual, never-married, childless woman who sang the praises of traditional womanhood, for which reason she is often dismissed by younger poets. A careful reading of her poetry and essays shows that this is a misrepresentation of her life and work. In this study I limit my reading of Mistral's work to poems specific to exile.

10. Gabriela Mistral, "Land of Absence," *Selected Poems of Gabriela Mistral,* trans. and ed. Doris Dana (Baltimore: Johns Hopkins Press, 1971), 82-85.

11. According to Antonio Skármeta, "Perspectiva de los novísimos," *Hispamérica* 10, no. 28 (1981): 64, writing in exile "is an emergency operation to recuperate the land that is its desired destination." Exile "breaks the ceremony of cultural identity. The exile faces the break and tries to repair it" (my translation).

12. Cristina Peri Rossi was born into a working-class family in Montevideo, Uruguay, in 1941. She published her first book, a collection of short stories called *Viviendo* (Living) in 1963. Peri Rossi taught literature, continued to write and publish (a novel, a book of poetry, more short stories), and was active in leftist politics until 1972, when the political situation forced her to leave the country. She has lived in Spain since that time, working as a journalist and solidifying her literary reputation, choosing to remain in exile even after the military dictatorship ended in Uruguay. All translations from Peri Rossi's works are my own.

13. Cristina Peri Rossi, "Las estatuas, o la condición del extranjero," *El museo de los esfuerzos inútiles* (Barcelona: Seix Barral, 1983).

14. Traba, *En cualquier lugar* (Bogotá: Siglo XXI, 1984).

15. Not all exile writers participate fully in this project. As I will suggest later in this chapter, the more alienated the writer was when living in her home country, the less desirable return becomes.

16. Rama, "Los contestarios del poder," discusses this phenomenon at some length.

17. To suggest that the painful experience of exile might have a positive side is to tread on sensitive territory, and this must be done respectfully and delicately. See, for example, Sosnowski, "Las otras fronteras." Before he begins his textual analysis, Sosnowski thoughtfully reminds the reader of how complicated the experience of exile is and cautions against broad generalizations that either damn or exalt the person who has gone into exile.

18. Luisa Valenzuela, *Como en la guerra* (Buenos Aires: Editorial Sudamericana, 1977). The English translation of this text, *He Who Searches,* was published in the United States in the volume *Strange Things Happen Here: 26 Short Stories and a Novel* (New York: Harcourt Brace Jovanovich, 1979). Valenzuela was born in Buenos Aires, Argentina, in 1938. She began writing as a journalist, perhaps in reaction to the highly imaginative work of her mother, the writer María Luisa Levinson. Between 1959 and 1961 she lived in Paris, where she reported for Argentine newspapers and wrote scripts for French television and radio. During the military dictatorship in Argentina, Valenzuela lived in New York City, writing and teaching in the creative writing program at Columbia University. Much of her work has been translated into English. Though Valenzuela is a prolific writer, in this chapter I confine my discussion to *Como en la guerra.*

19. Shortly after "confessing" in an interview to reading Lacan before she began to write *Como en la guerra,* Valenzuela states, "I'm not the keeper of truth nor do I pretend to be. That's why I foster ambiguity in my prose. The word is mine and possibly belongs to others, but not to everyone. So I invite you to read into that word whatever you will" (Garfield, *Women's Voices from Latin America,* 150). The parodic element of *Como en la guerra,* although not discussed in the present chapter, is not to be discounted.

20. Peri Rossi, from "Estado de exilio" in *Las voces distantes: Antología de los creadores uruguayos de la diáspora.* According to the short biographical note in this volume, *Estado de exilio* was given honorable mention for poetry by Casa de las Américas in 1979. This is the only reference I have seen to this volume. The poem cited seems to be the title poem of the collection.

21. The English translation unfortunately suppresses this name with its echoes of de Beauvoir's woman as "other."

22. In this construct of the tyrannized nation as both impregnable fortress and deadly labyrinth, doors are more a negative than a positive symbol. The transparent doors, reputed to lead to love and which seem to promise a way out, are tantalizingly inaccessible; the heavy dark ones serve only to imprison. This bleak view is shared by Gabriela Mistral in her poem "Puertas" (Doors), in which the threatening doors imprison occupants and shut out life (Mistral, 197-203). Mistral's house, like *la otra*'s, is an ambiguous place; the speaker does not know whether entering it will bring her ruin or salvation. Ultimately, the house emerges as a metaphor for life, which will be joyfully abandoned. As in Valenzuela's novel, Mistral's doors are finally felled to free those imprisoned by them. Mistral's is a religious solution to a spiritual problem: the doors come down when the speaker's freed soul rises in song with others. In *Como en la guerra* the problem is political, and the solution is more prosaic. Valenzuela's characters topple the doors with dynamite.

23. Peri Rossi, *Descripción de un naufragio* (Barcelona: Lumen, 1975).

24. Peri Rossi, "La influencia de Edgar Allan Poe en la poesía de Raimundo Arias," *La tarde del dinosaurio* (Barcelona: Planeta, 1976). In this story Peri Rossi plays on the popular wisdom that it is men who go into exile, leaving their less political women behind to take care of the children and keep the home fires burning. The wife is left behind, but only because she joins the underground resistance. It is deemed safer for the child and the ineffectual man to escape into exile, since the wife/mother's activities put them at jeopardy.

25. Nina Auerbach, *Woman and the Demon: The Life of a Victorian Myth* (Cambridge: Harvard University Press, 1982).

26. Perhaps not coincidentally, Peri Rossi links writing with forgetting and reading with the need to remember: "Escribo porque olvido / y alguien lee porque no evoca de manera / suficiente" (I write because I forget / and someone reads because he or she does not evoke sufficiently) [from *Lingüística general* (Editorial Prometeo, 1979), 13].

27. See Virginia Woolf, *Three Guineas* (New York: Harcourt, Brace, and World, 1938) for an excellent analysis of the citizen as male.

28. In another poem, "La otra," Mistral casts the double as a dangerous, life-threatening being who must be destroyed. Mistral's double is not figured outside the self, but within:

> I killed one in myself:
>
> I did not love her. (Mistral, 125; my translation)

The death of the double must be borne inside the speaker. The project of killing the angry, despairing side of the self is not entirely successful, however. The violent language of the poem and the speaker's vehement exhortation to other women to kill their own anger and despair belie the presumably achieved goal of inner peace. Furthermore, it is often the despairing other who gives voice and body to Mistral's own poetry.

The speaker of "La otra" is not an exile, and her conscious desire to destroy the double is an act of will.

29. The sudden evocation of this twin is such an obvious rhetorical device that her literal (textual) reality can be dismissed. Read this way, the twin is the revolutionary commitment *la otra* left behind, and the person she is protecting from the CIA is herself.

30. During the Franco era the Catalonian language was forbidden in public use and Castilian was imposed. There is now a resurgence of Catalonian in the schools, the media, and publishing.

31. Pedro Orgambide, "Oficio de narrador," *Hispamérica* 10, no. 30 (1981): 102.

32. Skármeta, "Perspectiva de los novísimos," says, "For writers, professionally imbued with the universe of language, a violent alteration of context reveals that verbal identity is not conferred only in local turns of speech but rather in a collective means of conceiving an existence wedged in tradition and language, which in turn determines the quality of reality" (62; my translation).

33. We are reminded, however, that Traba died after having written only one draft of *En cualquier lugar;* she had planned to rewrite it. See Elena Poniatowska, "Marta Traba o el salto por el vacío," *Revista Iberoamericana* 51, nos. 132-33 (1985): 883-97, especially 884-85. Traba, who was born in 1930 in Buenos Aires, made a name for herself as an art critic and professor in Colombia in the 1950s. In 1966 she published her first novel, *Ceremonias del verano* (Ceremonies of summer). Among her later works are *Los laberintos insolados* (Barcelona: Seix Barral, 1967); *Homérica latina* (Bogotá: C. Valencia Editores, 1979); and *Conversación al sur* (Mexico City: Siglo XXI, 1981). In the early 1980s Traba was living and working in the United States with her husband, Angel Rama. The Reagan government disapproved of their outspoken political views, and in 1983 denied them visas. Later that year, traveling from Spain to a conference in Colombia, their plane crashed and both Traba and Rama were killed.

34. Valenzuela, *Realidad nacional desde la cama* (Buenos Aires: Grupo Editor Latinoamericano, 1990).

4. Body/Politics

1. Alicia Partnoy, *The Little School: Tales of Disappearance and Survival in Argentina,* trans. Alicia Partnoy with Lois Athey and Sandra Braunstein (San Francisco: Cleis Press, 1986). The book's title comes from the military's ironic nickname for the center, *La Escuelita.* Neither education nor even reeducation was the goal of the Little School, unless the demand of the torturers for information could be deemed a desire to learn. The name Little School does betray the totalitarian (or authoritarian, pace Jeane Kirkpatrick) notion of school as a place of regimentation and strict obedience at the service of state ideology.

2. Fania Petzholdt and Jacinta Bevilacqua, *Nosotras también jugamos la vida: Testimonios de la mujer venezolana en la lucha clandestina 1948-1958* (Caracas: Editorial Ateneo de Caracas, 1979).

3. Jorge Narváez, "El testimonio 1972-1982: Transformaciones en el sistema literario," *Testimonio y literatura,* René Jara and Hernán Vidal, eds. (Edina, Minn.: Society for the Study of Contemporary Hispanic and Lusophone Revolutionary Literatures, 1986): 235-79, especially pages 250-51.

4. Moema Viezzer, *"Si me permiten hablar . . . " Testimonio de Domitila, una mujer de las minas de Bolivia* (Mexico City: Siglo XXI, 1977) and Elizabeth Burgos, *Me llamo Rigoberta Menchú, y así me nació la conciencia* (Mexico City: Siglo XXI, 1985). It is interesting to note that the English translation of Domitila Barrios's text by the leftist publishing company Monthly Review Press properly accords her the position of primary author and pays her the respect of utilizing her full name. It also transforms the title from a request to a demand: *Let Me Speak!*

5. See, for example, Doris Sommer, " 'Not Just a Personal Story': Women's *Testimonios* and the Plural Self," *Life/Lines: Theorizing Women's Autobiography,* Celeste Schenk and Bella Brodski, eds. (Ithaca: Cornell University Press, 1988), 107-30. Women's testimo-

nial literature has been a major topic for conference papers among such feminist critics of Latin American literature as Nancy Saporta Sternbach, Beth Jorgensen, Mary Jane Treacy, and Stacey Schlau. The academic organization Feministas Unidas sponsored a panel on the subject at the Modern Language Association meeting in 1987, and testimonial texts are increasingly turning up on women's studies syllabi.

6. Ariel Dorfman, "Código político y código literario: El género testimonio en Chile hoy," *Testimonio y literatura,* 170-234; see page 218.

7. At least one feminist reviewer of the book, Cristina Glendenning, does Partnoy the "favor" of saying that her book is really much too good to be called political. See *Hurricane Alice* 4, no. 1 (1987): 7.

8. Feminists writing in English whose analyses are based on this broad understanding of political structure tend to be either British Marxists or North American women of color. One exception is Elaine Tyler May, *Homeward Bound* (New York: Basic Books, 1988), a study of American Cold War ideology and the middle-class family.

9. Cristina Peri Rossi employs the same strategy in *Descripción de un naufragio,* a book of poems whose not-always-so-obvious referent is the crushing of the left in Uruguay. The final poem breaks the spell of poetic language, lists the names of some of the dead, and remands the reader to the newspapers for the rest of the story.

10. Renato Prada Oropeza, "De lo testimonial al testimonio: Notas para un deslinde del discurso-testimonio," *Testimonio y literatura.*

11. Dorfman, 194, my translation. The original text reads as follows: "este descuido por el lenguaje, el hecho de considerarlo como un mero vehículo de una verdad que ya está preestablecida, es decir, como un instrumento casi exterior a lo que es efectivamente importante, que tal manera de comprender la expresión hablada o escrita es una de las debilidades más definitivas de la izquierda chilena."

12. Dorfman, 192, mentions the anonymous text but gives no bibliographical citation.

13. The critics writing in *Testimonio y literatura* contradict each other in their efforts to pin the genre down. For René Jara, what makes testimonial writing closer to literature than to traditional historiography is the "I" of the writer. He finds testimony more material, less referential, and he claims that testimony breaks the barrier between public and private. Prada Oropeza claims that testimonial discourse is nonliterary in that it does not manipulate literary mechanisms, but Duquesne believes it is impossible to separate the literary from the nonliterary in testimonial writing because the literary is always at the service of the nonliterary. Cavalleri posits that the relationship to the referent is what distinguishes testimony from fiction, and then he goes on to problematize the nature of the referent itself in such a way that the distinction is muddied.

14. I refer here to the mainstream culture's approach to reading. Academic reading is quite another thing, though it is, if anything, more distancing. Feminist readers, on the other hand, stress the close connection between writing, reading, and lived experience. See, for example, Audre Lorde, "Poetry Is Not a Luxury," *Sister Outsider* (Trumansburg, N.Y.: The Crossing Press, 1984).

15. Tillie Olsen, *Silences* (New York: Delacorte Press/Seymour Lawrence, 1978); Susan Gubar, " 'The Blank Page' and the Issues of Female Creativity," *Critical Inquiry* 8 (winter 1981): 347-61.

16. Naomi Schor, "Female Paranoia: The Case for Psychoanalytic Feminist Criticism," *Yale French Studies,* 62 (1981): 204-19, quotation here from page 216.

17. The word for victim is a morphologically feminine noun, *la víctima.* The ambiguous relationship between grammatical gender and the sex/gender system, discussed in chapter 1, is well illustrated by this example. Though the feminine morphology of *víctima* does not

have an inherent semantic referent, the cultural meanings of both femininity and victimization come to reinforce each other in the confluence of meaning and morphology.

5. Gaby Brimmer

1. Elena Poniatowska and Gaby Brimmer, *Gaby Brimmer* (Mexico City: Editorial Grijalbo, 1979). All translations from this text are my own.

2. I use the term nonfiction not to claim truth-value but as a librarian's classification that includes history, biography, autobiography, ethnography, essay, and poetry.

3. The interdisciplinary collective Personal Narratives Group, which edited *Interpreting Women's Lives* (Bloomington: Indiana University Press, 1988), did explore the meaning of the terms it used.

4. My wavering between using Elena Poniatowska's full, first, or last name here is symptomatic of the merging of living person and literary personage discussed in this chapter.

5. Taken together, such scholarly work as the essays in *Testimonio y literatura*, René Jara and Hernán Vidal, eds.; Doris Sommer, " 'Not Just a Personal Story': Women's *Testimonios* and the Plural Self"; and Eliana Rivero, "Acerca del género 'Testimonio': Textos, narradores y 'artefactos,' " *Hispamérica* 16, nos. 46-47 (1987): 41-56, chronicles the emergence of testimony as a genre, complete with its own canon, list of characteristics, and awards. The critical work itself, of course, is a significant element in the process of claiming the existence of a new literary form.

6. Sylvia Molloy, "At Face Value: Autobiographical Writing in Spanish America," *Dispositio* 9, nos. 24-26 (1984): 1-18.

7. This is complicated by the fact that so many Mexican writers are urban and middle class, but they tend to take their material from the rural, mythic past, with a focus on the very poor or the very rich. An exception is the so-called Generation of 1963, which explores middle-class Mexico City.

8. Virginia Woolf, *A Room of One's Own* (New York: Harcourt, Brace, and World, 1929).

9. Linda Gordon uses this felicitous phrase as the title of her history of family violence, *Heroes of Their Own Lives: The Politics and History of Family Violence, Boston 1880-1960* (New York: Viking, 1988).

10. It is perhaps not entirely coincidental that the leftover bourgeois hegemony that is the purported target of this deconstructionist practice is better able to defend itself than are the already disempowered groups now on the verge of being able to claim an identity beyond that of other.

11. Octavio Paz, *El laberinto de la soledad*, 2d ed., revised and expanded (Mexico City: Fondo de Cultura Económica, 1959).

12. Gaby is even alienated from her Judaism, a fact that sometimes seems to disturb her, but which at other times she accepts as simply the way things are. Florencia claims her for Mexico and stresses Gaby's dislike of Jewish food, the one connection even the most assimilated Jews maintain to their culture.

13. A recent North American documentary features male care-givers who wax eloquent about their fulfillment working with disabled people in just the way that Florencia works with Gaby.

14. For a woman, "living one's own life" generally means living the prescribed life of getting married and having children. It is not clear that living out that scenario marks a woman as particularly free.

15. Carolyn Merchant, *The Death of Nature* (San Francisco: Harper and Row, 1980).

16. Susan Bordo, "The Cartesian Masculinization of Thought," *Signs: Journal of Women in Culture and Society* 11, no. 3 (spring 1986): 439-56, especially pages 441, 449, and 451.

17. Elaine Tyler May has suggested to me that Gaby's empowerment in Florencia's community may well derive from the fact that Florencia is empowered (financially well-off and not marginalized) there. Such shifting levels of empowerment and marginalization are a further indication of the relational nature of social reality and therefore subjectivity.

18. I am grateful to Cheri Register for pointing out to me that this is of special concern with cerebral palsy, where personal space cannot be defined, nor can one restrain oneself within it. The involuntary, spasmodic movements characteristic of cerebral palsy intrude on others' space.

19. This was the gist of Poniatowska's answer to my question about the extent of her collaboration with Gaby.

20. It is noteworthy that Gaby emerges in this text from a chorus of female voices. The men in her life are dead (her father Miguel), live far away (her uncle Otto), or have abandoned her (her brother David, her friend Luis).

21. Since the publication of *Gaby Brimmer,* Brimmer published a book of poetry.

22. Poniatowska, who was born in Paris in 1933 and came to Mexico at the age of nine, began her career as a journalist in 1953. Her first book, *Lilus Kikus,* is a collection of short stories. Her most celebrated works are a fruitful combination of journalism, history, and fiction that create difficulty for the literary taxonomer.

23. See, for example, *"Si me permiten hablar . . . " Testimonio de Domitila, una mujer de las minas de Bolivia,* whose sole designated author in the original Spanish version is the life historian, Moema Viezzer. In the English translation, entitled *Let Me Speak! Testimony of Domitila, a Woman of the Bolivian Mines,* Domitila Barrios, its subject, is listed as primary author, with help from Viezzer. Cynthia Steele has addressed some of these issues in "Committed Feminism and Feminist Commitment in the Criticism of Latin American Literature," paper presented at the International Conference of the Cultural Grounding of Hispanic and Luso-Brazilian Feminist Criticism, Minneapolis, March 31-April 2, 1988.

24. I am grateful to Riv-Ellen Prell for pointing this out to me, and for directing me to Vincent Crapanzano's *Tuhami,* which deals with this issue.

25. Here Poniatowska, the reporter, would seem to fall by the wayside, but she too participates in this desire to communicate. In the prologue she indicates that her motivation for collaborating on this book is connected to her sister's courage and persistence in working on the rehabilitation of a son who was severely injured and written off as a total loss by the medical community.

26. I refer here to Poniatowska's *Hasta no verte Jesús mío* (Mexico City: Biblioteca Era, 1969) and *Querido Diego, te abraza Quiela* (Mexico City: Ediciones Era, 1978).

6. The Uses and Limits of Foreign Feminist Theory

1. Elena Garro, *Los recuerdos del porvenir* (Mexico City: Joaquín Mortiz, 1963; Repr. Mexico City: Joaquín Mortiz and Secretaria de Educación Pública, 1985). All translations are from Elena Garro, *Recollections of Things to Come,* trans. Ruth L. C. Simms (Austin: University of Texas Press, 1986).

2. Julia Kristeva, "Women's Time," trans. Alice Jardine and Harry Blake, *Signs: Journal of Women in Culture and Society* 7 (1981): 13-35.

3. Julia Kristeva, *Revolution in Poetic Language,* trans. Margaret Walker, Intro. Leon S. Roudiez (New York: Columbia University Press, 1984). Although she has dealt with some literary texts, Kristeva has only very recently begun to consider the literature written by

women, and gender seems to be a minor issue for her when she does (her recent article on Marguerite Duras, commissioned by PMLA, is an example). The critics who look to Kristeva to understand the ways women writers might escape the confines of totalizing patriarchal language are probably closer in spirit to Hélène Cixous, for whom the unconscious theorized by Kristeva as the semiotic chora is a great repository of women's bodily knowledge. Adriana Méndez Rodenas, "Tiempo femenino, tiempo ficticio: *Los recuerdos del porvenir* de Elena Garro," *Revista Iberoamericana* 51 (1985): 843-51, relies heavily on Cixous. For an example of Kristeva as feminist theorist heroine, see Toril Moi, *Sexual/Textual Politics: Feminist Literary Theory* (New York: Methuen, 1985).

4. Basing her argument against the existence of the category "woman" on the questionability of gender identity, Kristeva cannot make the useful theoretical distinction between "women," the historical actors, and "woman," the abstract noun, both of which presuppose some form of gender identity. This is a problem for a feminism that includes an agenda for action.

5. The Mexican Revolution (1910-17) was fueled, in part, by anticlericalism. As a powerful landowner, the Church was perceived as a part of the oppressive system the revolutionary forces meant to overthrow. But in a profoundly Catholic country, there was bound to be a reaction to the wresting of power from the Church. The Cristeros were reactionary insofar as they opposed the revolution's reforms, but theirs was also a populist movement that cut across traditional class and rural/urban divisions. For some, supporting the Church's rights was a pretext for recovering their own power and privilege. For others the Cristero rebellion provided a means to oppose the excesses of the revolution and its rapid institutionalization.

6. Of the three temporal modalities —cyclical, monumental, and linear— presented in her essay "Women's Time," Kristeva associates the first two with both women's subjectivity and non-Western, primarily mystic, cultures, and attaches the third to a masculine and Eurocentric worldview. Kristeva attributes the term "monumental time" to Nietzsche and contrasts it to what he names "cursive time," i.e., what I follow Kristeva in calling "linear" or "historical" time (14).

7. García Márquez appears to have been so seduced and forewarned. The time structure of *100 Years of Solitude* owes much to Garro's *Recollections* and is similarly appealing (to the reader) and deadly (to the characters who cannot escape it).

8. See Frank Dauster, "Elena Garro y sus recuerdos del porvenir," *Journal of Spanish Studies: Twentieth Century* 8 (1980): 57-65; María Inés Fernández de Ciocca, "*Los recuerdos del porvenir* o la novela del tiempo," *Revista Interamericana de Bibliografía* 36 (1986): 39-51; and Magda Portal, *Proceso narrativo de la revolución mexicana* (Madrid: Espasa-Calpe, 1980), 258-70, for discussions of narrative voice in *Recuerdos*.

9. Not only the town, but also several of its inhabitants have access to the knowledge that monumental time allows. Martín Moncada, his daughter Isabel, and his sons Juan and Nicolás all, to some extent, live in, and know through, monumental time.

10. Dust is the form stone takes just before memory blows away. Toward the end of the novel Isabel lies still and feels herself filling with dust as her sense of herself as a subject with a past and future erodes.

11. The riddle of the disappearance of the sacristan and the reason for the soldier Damián Alvarez's death exemplify these, respectively.

12. What for the contemporary reader, living in linear time, happens in a linear way (the reading of chapters is a sequential activity), "in fact" all goes on at once. So does the printed word both abet and preclude simultaneity.

13. Garro is without a doubt a sophisticated and cosmopolitan writer, who, though born in Puebla (1920), has spent most of her adult life in France. Her experiments with time

and knowledge in the novel are derived from an education infused with European high culture and her participation in an aesthetic milieu that is as Continental as it is indigenous. Mexico's culture is mestizo, and, unlike her character Elvira Montúfar, Garro is not about to disclaim her indigenous ancestry. But though she is sympathetic to them Garro does silence the Indians in her novel, and insofar as she represents a moment in Mexican history, the Cristero rebellion, she misrepresents it by casting it as a primarily middle-class movement.

14. This notion of words as containing value in themselves, even as being corporeal, is reiterated in the madness of Juan Cariño, the wise fool, who in the evenings goes through the streets of Ixtepec capturing harmful words that have been spoken throughout the day, and by Isabel who comes to recognize the depth of her lover's betrayal when she sees before her her own words of accusal. It is interesting to note, in this vein, that Mistral and Peri Rossi have written poems on the danger of the word made material, the former in "Una palabra" and the latter in a poem where a woman hurls the poet's words around the room.

15. The problem with this, and the reason why Kristeva is so often "misread" as claiming the semiotic as the feminine, is that its counterpart, the symbolic, is characterized as the realm of language, logic, and the paternal. As these phenomena are coded masculine in culture (in fact may be taken to *be* culture) what is left for their opposite is the maternal and the feminine. Kristeva maintains that the presymbolic, pre-Oedipal maternal is not gendered, but although that may be the infant's perception, it is not the adult's. The chaos and security of the semiotic are precisely what Western culture ascribes to the sexual and maternal faces of femininity. Kristeva recognizes this and warns that for women to exalt the semiotic as their space is to risk embracing their own oppression.

16. It should be made clear that while Kristeva praises modernist writers like Joyce for pushing the semiotic to the surface of the text, she does not recommend that the general public abandon the symbolic realm. Total immersion in the semiotic is madness. Garro's Juan Cariño, who lives in the (debased) maternal/sexual realm of the whorehouse, and for whom language does not "mean" but "is," is a case in point.

17. The English version of this phrase, "what looks like a stone," represses the tension of an oddly modified subject, an "apparent stone." "What looks like a stone" balances the subject (what) against that which it looks like, but is not. A "piedra aparente" is in a perpetual state of instability between the noun and its modifier.

18. Margaret Homans, "A Feminine Tradition," *Women Writers and Poetic Identity: Dorothy Wordsworth, Emily Brontë, and Emily Dickinson* (Princeton: Princeton University Press, 1980), 215-36, discusses the woman-as-rock metaphor in English-language poetry by women from Dorothy Wordsworth and Emily Dickinson to Sylvia Plath and Adrienne Rich, and points out that "a woman, fortunately, can be a rock only in a poem; language's difference saves this poetics from itself" (236). Ixtepec is not all that sure.

19. This world of sibling perfection is echoed in Rosa and Rafaela, the twin lovers of Lieutenant Colonel Cruz, who eventually exclude him from their bed.

20. Joanna Russ's pioneering article, "What Can a Heroine Do?, or, Why Women Can't Write," *Images of Women in Fiction: Feminist Perspectives,* Susan Koppelman Cornillon, ed. (Bowling Green, Ohio: Bowling Green University Popular Press, 1972), explains the mechanism by which Gregoria interprets Isabel's fate. Within the novel the conundrum of women's speech is expressed by the double bind in which the combination of Doña Elvira's unguarded speech and her daughter Conchita's silence undermines the plot to distract Rosas while the Cristeros assemble.

21. Even the most sophisticated readings of this novel have accepted Gregoria's word about Isabel's fate. Of these, the most compelling is Jean Franco's, who writes: "Women do not enter history—only romance. Either they are legends like Julia, the elusive phantom of

male desire, or like Isabel they are the undesired surrogates who are not objects of desire but who allow themselves to be seduced by power. Such women do not wrest interpretive power from the masters and are not commemorated by posterity, except as traitors to the community that has been forever bonded by memory and speech. The fact that Isabel's treachery becomes inscribed in stone while Julia's legend remains a legend only underlines the fact that both are outside history" (*Plotting Women*, 138). The memory and speech that bond community in this novel are, as the madman Juan Cariño knows, treacherous. See also Sandra Boschetto, "Romancing the Stone in Elena Garro's *Los recuerdos del porvenir*," *Journal of the Midwest Modern Language Association* (fall, 1989): 1-11. For a discussion of why readers continue to accept Gregoria's story, see my "Residual Authority and Gendered Resistance," *Critical Theory, Cultural Politics and Latin American Narrative*, Steven Bell et al., eds. (Notre Dame, Ind.: University of Notre Dame Press, forthcoming).

22. As an outsider like Julia, Felipe Hurtado is necessarily mysterious and unknowable. He is a seductive figure, offering escape not only to Julia, but to the Moncadas, who give him lodging. Hurtado animates the Moncada household by mounting a play. The rehearsals for the performance of this play become increasingly important for Isabel, as if this creation of something out of nothing were itself a rehearsal for creative action beyond the simulacrum of theater.

7. Sylvia Molloy's Lesbian Cartographies

1. The added twist of incest simply pushes the possibility further beyond the pale.

2. Sylvia Molloy, *En breve cárcel* (Barcelona: Seix Barral, 1981); *Certificate of Absence*, trans. Daniel Balderston (Austin: University of Texas Press, 1989). Though Balderston's name is on the translation, Molloy worked with him on it. All translations cited here are from this edition, unless otherwise noted. An early version of this chapter appeared in *Cultural and Historical Grounding for Hispanic and Luso-Brazilian Feminist Literary Criticism*, Hernán Vidal, ed.

3. Furthermore, she is not locked into rigid gender categories: in her dreams the writer becomes a boy or identifies with male figures in nonsexual situations.

4. The analogy goes further. Bonnie Zimmerman, in "What Has Never Been: An Overview of Lesbian Feminist Criticism," *Making a Difference*, Coppélia Kahn and Gayle Green, eds. (New York: Methuen, 1985), 177-210, cites Susan Wolfe as saying that "lesbian literature is characterized by the use of the continuous present, unconventional grammar and neologism; and . . . it breaks boundaries between art and the world, between events and our perceptions of them, and between past, present and the dream world" (195). This description of lesbian narrative is remarkably like descriptions of the contemporary Latin American novel. See, for example, Francine Masiello's discussion of the characteristics of Argentine narrative in "*En breve cárcel*, la producción del sujeto," *Hispamérica* 14, no. 41 (August 1985): 103-12. Insofar as the broad categories—lesbian writing and Latin American writing—derive from late-twentieth-century cultures in a conscious process of creating themselves within complex and often painful political circumstances, it is not surprising that they have found similar formal solutions.

5. Since lesbianism is disobedience it is a handy metaphor for disruption and social change; cf. Reina Roffé's *Monte de Venus* (Buenos Aires: Corregidor, 1976). Lesbianism as defiance of patriarchy, however, is a subtext at best in *En breve cárcel*, where the protagonist unpeels layers of her psyche in a self-exploration (though she denies that is her aim) stripped as thoroughly as possible of social/cultural/historical context. Julia Penelope Stanley's description of the prefeminist lesbian novel fits Molloy's text in an almost uncanny way: "the lesbian character creates for herself a mythology of darkness, a world in which she moves

through dreams and shadows" [from "Uninhabited Angels: Metaphors for Love," *Margins* 23 (1975), quoted in Zimmerman, p. 194] See also Wolfe, "Stylistic Experimentation in Millett, Johnston and Wittig," unpublished paper, presented at annual conference of the Modern Laguage Association, 1978.

6. Though the narrator says the writer would again grow up in the city of her birth given the choice, she does not indicate that she wishes to return there.

7. This is not to suggest that the heterosexual female body is unproblematic in its over-determinedness. Heterosexual women must also reclaim their own sexuality, in order to get beyond being relegated to it. *Los recuerdos del porvenir* takes the reification of women's sexuality to its limit, turning it to stone and taking the life from it. *Como en la guerra*, on the other hand, pushes beyond the limit. AZ's scientific method is insufficient to take all of *la otra* into account; he is unable to turn her into the stuff of a study. *La otra* refuses to stay within the boundaries of pure (i.e., accessible, degraded, contained) sexuality drawn around the prostitute. She escapes from both AZ and his text by occupying the space of the whore so fully that she finally bursts it, leaving behind the skeletal remains of her masterful performance: a few violently sadistic photographs that are, ultimately, representations less of her body than of the pornographic mind itself.

8. Cheri Register, in *Living with Chronic Illness: Days of Patience and Passion* (New York: MacMillan Free Press, 1987) describes this phenomenon. Register's book documents the control chronically ill people come to experience over their illness when they can, in Register's words, name the unhealthy self.

9. This fear of disintegration is figured throughout the novel, in both dream and memory. In one instance, the writer recalls the accident that killed her father and her aunt, with emphasis on their broken bodies.

10. Martha Noel Evans, *Masks and Tradition: Women and Politics in 20th Century France* (Ithaca: Cornell University Press, 1987), 185, uses an almost identical metaphor in a way that helps explain the fascination and repulsion we see in this text toward the flayed body: "One might say that the mask of male discourse adheres to the female body; when the mask is dismantled, the body parts come with it."

11. Monique Wittig, *The Lesbian Body,* trans. Peter Owen (New York: Wm. Morrow, 1975; reprint, Boston: Beacon Press, 1986), 17.

12. This play between physical enclosure and mental unboundedness was earlier enacted by Emily Dickinson, one of whose poems gives the English version of this novel its name. See, for example, Suzanne Juhasz, *The Uncharted Continent* (Bloomington: Indiana University Press, 1981).

13. The affirmative value of skin is underscored in the scene where the writer finally sleeps with Renata and the primary body reference is to the lover's skin: "Nunca tocó una piel, la piel de otro, como esa noche" (55) [She never touched a skin, the skin of another, as she did that night (my translation)].

14. Either too clever or not clever enough, I was thrown off by the mention of White Plains, which in both my memory and my atlas is a suburb not of Buffalo but of New York City.

15. Molloy, in "Sentido de ausencias," *Revista Iberoamericana* 51, nos. 132-33 (July-December 1985): 483-88, an essay on the absence of women writers in her life, writes that she will make sure in the future to be aware of the women writers who preceded her and accompany her. The verb Molloy uses to bid them to her, *convocar*, is the same one that the writer in *En breve cárcel* uses when she acknowledges her need for her mother and sister: "Es hora—o por lo menos lo es para mí—de reconocerme en una tradición que, sin que yo lo supiera del todo, me ha estado respaldando. No sólo eso; es hora de contribuir a convocarla en cada letra que escribo" (488, emphasis added) ["It is time—or at least it is for

me—to recognize myself within a tradition that, without my entirely knowing about it, has been undergirding me. It is not only that; it is time to contribute to summoning it in each letter I write" (my translation)].

16. The impossibility of reaching "Ephesus" is crucial to the writer's growing integrity and healing, insofar as there are strong, though repressed, indications in the text that the relationship between the writer and her father was incestuous. This aspect of the novel was brought to my attention by my students at the University of Minnesota.

17. Molloy was born in Buenos Aires in 1938, studied in Paris, and later moved to the United States.

18. As a prominent critic, Molloy is something of a public personage whose other published works also cast light on this novel. Her writer sits in a room forging this text, but what she meant to be doing was a safely distanced scholarly study of autobiography. As far as we know, the writer never wrote that piece, but Molloy did. She presented it to the Department of Romance Languages at the University of Michigan in 1984, which subsequently published it in its journal, *Dispositio*. See Molloy, "At Face Value: Autobiographical Writing in Spanish America," *Dispositio* 9, nos. 24-26 (1984): 1-18. In 1991 Molloy published her book (with the same title as her essay) on Latin American autobiography.

19. Molloy, "At Face Value," 3.

20. Ocampo, founder and publisher of the influential literary journal *Sur*, was a key figure in the debates around twentieth-century Argentine culture. According to Molloy, "Victoria Ocampo, in her *Autobiografía* (1979-83), . . . aspires to construct a figure, a *persona* representative of woman's role in Argentina at a given time" ("At Face Value" 3).

21. I am not claiming some biologically determined way of understanding the self, divided forever along gender lines. In fact, I believe that issues of identity presented in this novel are also influenced by male writers: Molloy's 1982 article on Felisberto Hernández's autobiographical text, *Diario del sinvergüenza*, brings up some of the issues of the problems of the unified self. She quotes Hernández: "He andado buscando mi propio yo desesperadamente como alguien que quisiera agarrarse el alma con una mano que no es de él" ["*Tierras de la memoria:* La entreapertura del texto," *Escritura* 7, nos.13-14 (Caracas, January-December 1982): 69]. It is also likely that Molloy's close reading of Borges has also made some mark on her thinking: "esa certeza de que no hay 'yo de conjunto'" (ibid.). She resolves the problem of the instability of the self differently from the way Borges and Hernández do, however.

22. Molloy, *At Face Value: Autobiographical Writing in Spanish America.*

8. Cristina Peri Rossi and the Question of Lesbian Presence

1. On the relationship between sexual freedom and political freedom, Peri Rossi states: "Yo creo que en realidad la revolución política y la sexual van muy unidas desde el momento en que las formas de la sexualidad en una sociedad determinada corresponden a un modo de producción económica y a los roles culturales, educativos y sociales que la clase dirigente establece como "normales", esto es, los más frecuentes. . . . La revolución tiene que pasar necesariamente por la libertad sexual (solamente limitada por el derecho individual de cada uno a no ser violentado en sus deseos) y por la liberación completa y absoluta de la mujer, pero para ello es necesario que se vea la relación que existe entre la dominación y los roles sexuales, entre la sociedad capitalista y la esclavitud de la mujer" [I believe that in reality political revolution and sexual revolution are very close, from the moment when the forms of sexuality in a given society correspond to a means of economic production and to the cultural, educational, and social roles that the ruling class establishes as "normal," that is, the most common. . . . Revolution necessarily has to pass through sexual freedom

(limited only by the individual's right not to be violated in his or her desires) and through the complete and absolute liberation of women, but for that it's necessary to see the relation that exists between domination and gender roles, between capitalist society and the slavery of women].

On feminism: "En cuanto a la condición femenina, estoy convencida de que se trata de una esclavitud ligada al sistema de producción económica mundial, que se atenúa indudablemente bajo el socialismo, sin llegar a desaparecer del todo, evolución que tardará muchísimos siglos aun, cuando todo se cambie, especialmente, se cambie la necesidad de atribuir roles al individuo, roles sexuales, roles económicos, roles psicológicos, etc." [As far as the status of women is concerned, I am convinced that it is about a kind of slavery connected to the system of world economic production, that it is indubitably attenuated under socialism, without disappearing altogether, an evolution that will take many centuries still, when everything has changed, especially the need to attribute roles to the individual, sex roles, economic roles, psychological roles, etc.]. These comments are from an interview with Peri Rossi in Eileen Zeitz, "Tres escritores uruguayos en el exilio," *Chasqui* 9, no. 1 (November 1979): 79-87, especially page 82. All translations from the article are my own.

2. In this vein it is interesting to note that Peri Rossi's prose, which is little concerned with overtly lesbian material, is far more available than her poetry, where lesbianism is a more obvious presence.

3. It is telling that Peri Rossi chooses to use the word "homosexual" rather than "lesbian." Jacqueline Zita (personal conversation) pointed out that this choice suggests a love of likeness within existing, heterosexist structures, while the term "lesbian" indicates a refusal of the structures themselves. Though in this chapter I continue to refer to all of Peri Rossi's representations of woman-with-woman eroticism as lesbian, Zita's distinction suggests ways in which my analysis can be taken further.

4. Also, Peri Rossi expects a heterosexist reader, at least in her early works. For example, *Viviendo*, (Montevideo: Alfa, 1963), in which the disguised lover turns out to be a woman, "works" only if the reader reads that figure as male.

5. Peri Rossi, "Génesis de *Europa después de la lluvia*" *Studi di letteratura ispanoamericano* 13-14 (1983): 63-78. Translations from this article are mine.

6. Peri Rossi, "Génesis de *Europa después de la lluvia*," 77-78.

7. Peri Rossi, *Europa después de la lluvia* (Madrid: Fundación Banco Exterior, 1987); *Evohé* (Montevideo: Ed. Girón, 1971).

8. John F. Deredita, "Desde la diáspora: entrevista con Cristina Peri Rossi," *Texto Crítico* 9 (1978), 121-142. Translation is my own.

9. I am grateful to Cheryl Kader (personal conversation) for this insight. Monique Wittig, rejecting the idea that lesbians are women at all, in their refusal of traditional gender behavior, moves even further in this direction than Peri Rossi. Wittig, however, is attentive to the ways language reinscribes gender difference and is therefore linguistically iconoclastic, but Peri Rossi is maddening (to me, at least) in persisting in her use of a masculinist language that renders women invisible.

10. Arlene Raven and Ruth Iskin, "Through the Peephole: Toward a Lesbian Sensibility in Art," *Women and Values: Readings in Recent Feminist Philosophy*, Marilyn Pearsall, ed. (Belmont, Calif.: Wadsworth Publishing Co., 1986), 257-61. Raven and Iskin point out that work produced by isolated lesbians will differ from that created within a supportive community: "Lesbian expressions that are created in isolation often reflect the antipathy of patriarchal culture toward lesbianism. These are no less powerful or articulate statements of the lesbian experience, but the lesbian experience lived and expressed by a lesbian who is isolated in a heterosexist environment differs from that of the lesbian/feminist who is supported by a lesbian/feminist community" (258).

11. This can also be read as a realigning of gender and sexuality. In Peri Rossi's most recent novel, *Solitario de amor* (Barcelona: Grijalbo, 1988), a tale of sexual obsession, the heterosexual male narrator evokes a nonphallic eroticism. He longs not to penetrate and possess, but rather to merge with and dissolve into the woman he desires. This positing of a new form of male heterosexuality is in keeping with Peri Rossi's deconstruction of gender along sexual lines.

12. Peri Rossi also associates Sappho with Borges, no doubt the single most attacked-for-not-being-political writer in Latin America.

13. Susanna Ragazzoni, "La escritura como identidad: Una entrevista con Cristina Peri Rossi," *Studi di letteratura ispano-americana* 15-16 (1983): 227-41 .

14. If language is not transparent (as Peri Rossi well knows it is not), then an argument can be made asserting that any use of language carries with it the need for the assumption (rather than the simple expression) of a voice. This argument, however, is not entirely convincing in Peri Rossi's case, where evasion seems deliberate.

15. Note, here, the demands of the skin, the organ so central to Sylvia Molloy's recuperation of the lesbian body.

16. Peri Rossi, *Diáspora* (Barcelona: Lumen, 1976).

17. The Alice in Wonderland theme recurs as a motif in the work of more than one contemporary Latin American woman writer, including Albalucía Angel (*Dos veces Alicia*), Claribel Alegría (*Luisa en Realityland*), and Ana Lydia Valdéz, (*Después de Alicia*).

18. Peri Rossi, *Una pasión prohibida* (Barcelona: Seix Barral, 1986); *La nave de los locos* (Barcelona: Seix Barral, 1984); *Solitario de amor* (Barcelona: Grijalbo, 1988); *Cosmoagonías* (Barcelona: Laia, 1988).

19. This is the only place I am aware of in Peri Rossi's work where she pays much attention to pronouns and gender meanings. See Monique Wittig, "The Mark of Gender," *Feminist Issues* 5, no. 2 (1985): 3-12.

20. At least one other text by Peri Rossi also connects lesbianism to activist politics: the poem from *Lingüística general* cited on pages 223-24, in which the relationship between the speaker and her lover is called subversive.

Index

Akhmatova, Anna, 55
Angel, Albalucía, xi, 156 n17
Auerbach, Nina, 38
author/text relationship, 73-74, 116;
    authenticity and, 117; autobiography
    and, 61, 111-14, 118; poet/speaker
    relationship and, 121, 124, 131-32;
    testimonial writing and, 57

Barrios de Chungara, Domitila, 48, 146
    n4, 149 n23
body: disability and, 62-70, 76, 149 n18;
    gender and, 6, 78; lesbian, 97-106,
    108, 116; politics and, xv, 49, 54;
    sexuality and, 66-67; writing and, 98,
    104-6, 123
body/mind split, 18, 53-54, 67-68, 75,
    100
Bordo, Susan, 68
Brimmer, Gaby, 17, 61-76, 114; *Gaby
    Brimmer,* 60-76, 77

Cartagena, Teresa de, 21
Cixous, Hélène, 7, 11, 23, 89, 150 n3
class, 16, 63-64, 69, 72-73, 86, 115. *See
    also* gender

criticism, feminist, 19, 117; Latin
    American literature and, xi-xvi, 26, 49,
    78, 90; lesbian theory and, xiv;
    literary taxonomy and, 60-61; Marxist
    criticism and, 23; prescription and, 19,
    117; psychoanalytic, xiii, 20, 23, 26,
    27, 63, 78, 91. *See also* criticism, Latin
    American feminist; criticism, lesbian;
    feminism; theory, feminist
criticism, Latin American, xi, xiv-xvi, 18,
    97
criticism, Latin American feminist, xiv, 9,
    12, 20, 26, 59, 115, 135, 142 n9. *See
    also* criticism, feminist
criticism, lesbian, 116

Daly, Mary, 11
de Lauretis, Teresa, 2, 13, 139 n3
Dickinson, Emily, 108, 114, 153 n12
Dorfman, Ariel, 52, 56, 147 n11

Evans, Martha Noel, 153 n10
exile, 27, 29-46, 108, 117, 119, 143 n7;
    as metaphor, 27, 46, 142 n12;
    language and, 30, 42-43, 46;
    lesbianism and, 40-41, 98, 114, 130-
    34; men and, 36, 39; women and,

Amy Kaminsky is associate professor of women's studies at the University of Minnesota. She is the editor of *Flores del Agua/Waterlilies: An Anthology of Spanish Women Writers from the Fifteenth to the Nineteenth Centuries* (forthcoming from Minnesota) and has written extensively on problems of the body, text, and gender in Spanish and Latin American literatures.